In Gratitude Judy Berg

Imagine Your Soul Abundant

*Attracting success, fulfillment
and true happiness.*

Judy Berg

UPSTART
PRESS

ISBN 987-0-9783774-0-3

Printed and bound in Canada

UpStart Press
829 Norwest Road, Suite 335
Kingston, ON   K7P 2N3
www.upstartpress.ca

Dedicated to my loving parents
Anne and Doug
whose lives model their favorite saying ...

"There is a truth that makes us brothers,
None goes this way alone,
That which we put out into the lives of others,
Comes back into our own."
     – author unknown

Contents

Acknowledgements

Imagine Your Soul Abundant: Attracting Success, Fulfillment, and True Happiness is my personal testimony to the Law of Attraction in action. As the German philosopher Goethe said, "Whatever you dream, begin it! Boldness has genius, power and magic." So I did. I committed to my dream to present these ideas to as many people as I could and all kinds of magical and wonderful things began to happen!

I am a student of quantum energy, human consciousness, spirituality, applied kinesiology, intuition, and the Law of Attraction. I see the interconnectedness of the concepts. By weaving these ideas together, I intend to save you the hours of extensive research it took for me to discover these interconnections!

When I find something that works, I feel compelled to share it in hopes it will have the same positive impact on your life. My intention is not only to inspire and challenge you but, also to provide you with the "how-to" make a life transformation. What is original and exciting is revealing the symbiotic nature of many great thoughts. The presentation of these intersecting pieces takes you from just reading the concepts to actually transforming yourself through the techniques and applications.

I am grateful to my colleagues in Alberta who recognized my passion for this subject and inspired me to develop my first Attracting Success seminar on the Law of Attraction. In particular, I wish to thank Dennis and Nicki Goff, whose belief in the project and volunteer assistance on a professional graphic design enabled me to pursue my dream to teach. The list of seminar participants and friends who have supported me over the years is too long to include, but many of you will see yourselves and the stories you shared in this work. I am grateful for your belief and support. Special thanks to David VanAmburg and the folks at Mutual Gravity for guiding me through the world of the Internet, manifesting my dream to develop a website, and encouraging me in the presentation of this material. To Patrick Hiller, whose creative genius on the graphic designs of the book and website make me proud to put this product on the market. To Kim Burney, for all her help, patience and joint venture relationship in our online courses, now and into the future. Additionally, some special people who read the early versions of the manuscript and whose feedback and encouragement inspired me to go forward: Truus and Alfons Claassen, Jim McElroy, RitaSue Bolton, Sunshower Rose, David VanAmburg, Jim Berg, Kim Burney and, notably, Blythe Bohonos whose enthusiastic dedication to the creative process, as well as the content, kept me buoyed throughout. My appreciation to the editor and publisher I attracted! —Christina Decarie at Peony Creative and UpStart Press. I am deeply grateful, not only for the incredible editing done by my daughter, Markail, but for the special opportunity it gave us to create together—as we birthed this book—she also birthed her first child, our first grandchild, Nicholas John—and to her husband, Stuart, for his support and patience! I save to the last, two special men in my life—my son, Regan, for whom it has been an honor and a privilege to be his mother—and my husband, Jim, who showed me what it means to live in non-duality. His unconditional love is a model for what can be accomplished if an entire planet were living in the light of highest consciousness. I AM the most abundant, successful, fulfilled, and truly happy woman on the planet—through the blessings of my family and friends.

Inviting all who
seek life's abundance ...

We are not creatures of circumstances; we are creators of circumstances.
  – Benjamin Disraeli

Imagine your Soul Abundant! Success, fulfillment, and true happiness are waiting. You can have it all!

You are about to learn how to create the abundance you seek through the exploration of a natural law of the universe, its foundations in quantum physics, and its connection to ancient teaching and prophecy. The natural law we are referring to is the Law of Attraction. This law is playing a significant part in the success, or lack of the success, you are currently experiencing!

Perhaps you are happy with what you have achieved but have a feeling there must be more to life than this. Or, you are just exhausted by the stress of the day-to-day grind. Whatever your reasons for being attracted to this book, I expect you are at least curious about the possibility of a different life experience.

Promises of abundance and riches reverberate throughout the self-help world. Many have pursued these promises only to become discouraged trying to figure out how to make them work! Positive thinking or goal setting alone will not get you what you desire — there is something more.

The Soul Abundant approach is a proven way to achieve success and material gain through understanding the Law of Attraction, but there is something to be acquired that is way more profound. Being self-absorbed in the pursuit of happiness and using personal gain as the sole measuring stick for success is all too common. Did you know that tens of thousands of clients sought out Edgar Cayce for readings, all wanting to have their future successes revealed but NOT ONE asked him to forecast on their role or their relationship to the well-being of the world! True wealth and success does mean having it all —personal, family, community, and global! Accessing phenomenal success and abundance comes through attaining inner peace and happiness. In pursuing higher levels of consciousness, we project that consciousness outward, contributing to the good of all. It is in this process that we create and reap life's real trove of abundance — Being at One with ourselves and humanity.

Success, then, is about "BEING MORE" and less about "DOING MORE." The quest to becoming SOUL ABUNDANT is a way to achieve success in alignment with one's beingness — one's life purpose or higher consciousness — and the greater good.

Throughout the book is evidence that science is proving we are the creators of our reality. There are discoveries of the mysteries of ancient prophecies heralding the time for evolution to higher consciousness is now, and new revelations in science and spirituality that are reuniting to remind us of our Oneness. The Law of Attraction gives us insights to the next evolutionary step. Most important is the awakening to an idea whose time has come. You and your Higher Self are being called upon to co-create a different future.

We are living in what the Greeks called 'Kairos' — the right moment
— for a metamorphosis of the gods...
     – C.G. Jung

In the first segment, "Why is the Law of Attraction a law," we engage in an introductory discussion on the science behind the Law of Attraction (quantum physics) to explain why this law works all the time. "Prophecies and duality" explores fascinating prophecies of the ancients, in particular, the ancient Mayans, whose calendars of evolution of consciousness may explain why there is so much interest in the Law of Attraction at this time.

Each of the last segments, "BE – Intention," "HAVE – Transcending Consciousness," and "DO – Inspired, Intuitive Action," is part of a three-step process to master the Law of Attraction, learning to attract more rewarding and higher consciousness experiences.

The time to mature into the loving, abundant creatures of our destiny is now! Success, fulfillment, and true happiness await you.

Are you ready to join in this pursuit — right now?

Why is the Law of Attraction a law?

How is an individual mind able to resonate its pattern to another mind? One would certainly feel a new awareness. Is this cosmic consciousness? Is this what is happening now to so many? I believe the answer is 'yes'. We are beginning a new age of awareness, the age of quantum consciousness, the age of the conscious atom. By looking within ourselves, we may be able to solve the problems facing us on the final frontier — the frontier of the human spirit.
– Dr. Fred Alan Wolfe, Taking the Quantum Leap

1
What's the buzz?

What's all this fuss about abundance, success, higher consciousness, and the Law of Attraction? Where is this coming from? Why now?

Throughout history, people have searched for meaning and purpose. Now, amazing discoveries in science are bringing scientific and spiritual philosophies into alignment, helping us to better understand life's purpose and our relationships to each other. Driving this movement to reuniting science and spirituality is quantum mechanics. Just think! Scientific thought separated us from a sense of purpose or meaning, and now, it is through new discoveries in quantum science, we are being presented with a profoundly new spiritual way of BEING in the world!

Much of the buzz can be linked to atomic discoveries in the early part of the twentieth century. Scientists split the atom into subatomic parts, expecting to see smaller and smaller particles. What they discovered astounded them. At the smallest level it was not a particle but a wave. It was energy! But wait a minute! One moment it was energy, the next moment it was a particle! Matter is energy or energy is matter! How bizarre! The physical world we think exists does not exist at all! It is instead a mass of rapidly moving molecules changing in form depending on the expectations of whoever is looking at it!

If the Observer is determining form...if the Observer is creating reality...then the Observer is an interconnected piece of the end result! The Observer and the Observed are connected and influencing each other to determine what will unfold! There truly is no "in here" or "out there."

If that is happening at the micro level is it possible to use this model to explain life at the macro level? It was several decades after the initial discoveries of the nature of the subatomic before implications for human consciousness were explored.

Can you wrap your mind around all this? You are energy, interconnected with all other energy fields, and you are determining reality through your expectations! There is no separation between Observer, matter or energy. Quantum physics is unveiling an extraordinary truth, a truth of energy frequencies continuously weaving through all things, animate and inanimate. As the Observer, we create — our past, present and future.

This way of being emphasizes our interconnectivity and reconnects with our identity or purpose. Ancient spiritual avatars taught we are all brothers and part of something greater than the physical body walking on the planet. Discoveries in quantum physics are now proving the truth of the spiritual messages of those prophets, mystics, and sages.

There is value in looking back in time, not only to see how far we have come in understanding who we are and why are we here, but also to realize there is still so much to discover. Astonishingly, a mere 500 years ago, nothing more than a nanosecond in the estimated 14 billion–year history of the planet, everyone believed the world was flat. Today we know the world is round. If we had it so wrong about the "flat-world stuff" for all those years, is it possible there are other ideas or beliefs as incorrect as a flat earth? How many other life-changing truths are yet to be revealed?

The Law of Attraction is one such life-changing concept arising out of quantum physics awareness that the universe is a huge sea of energy. In that sea, as Wallace Wattles said almost 100 years ago, prior to the discovery of quantum physics,

> There is a thinking stuff from which all things are made and which in its original state permeates, penetrates, and fills the interspaces of the universe. A thought in this substance produces the thing that is imaged by the thought.

Our connection with this "thinking stuff," how we transform this energy into thought, which then, manifests into reality is explained through the Law of Attraction. There are no empty spaces. The universe is a teeming mass of energy from which all creation arises from the divine "thinking stuff." Quantum physics confirms this connection to the energy field.

Not only is this is mind-boggling, it is the path to a new way of experiencing our world.

2

A new way of being

Most humans try to change things by focusing on behaviors. They keep thinking they can make things better by doing something. So everyone is running around trying to figure out what they can do. The focus is on doing something, rather than on believing something.
– Neale Donald Walsh

Achieving greater results means we participate in the creative process by raising our vibration and consciousness to higher levels. We BECOME MORE. We fulfill a plan of evolution. Every thought is a creation. Every creation is an evolution, evolving from thought through to manifestation of reality. The process of creation of the universe is not completed! We are not yet completed! Our role in this ongoing evolution process is to attain higher levels of ethics, spirituality, and consciousness.

I am often asked, "Does this mean life for someone who has mastered the Law of Attraction is just a bed of roses — that negative things never happen?" Let's hope not. That would defeat why we are here on this planet. We are here to learn life lessons and to reach for ever-higher levels of consciousness, individually and collectively. Always in our darkest moments lies the potential for greatness and growth, if we choose to see it. Can we believe when these dark nights of the Soul visit us we are being given an opportunity for quantum growth? As we personally achieve higher consciousness, we collectively move to higher and higher states of being. Everything in the process of creation is in motion. That is evolution and that is what makes us co-creators, and advances civilization towards its full potential.

When you first start to work with the Law of Attraction, you may be more interested in knowing how you can attract the car you want, the romance you want or the career you want. You start out being more concerned about getting more of the things you want in your life. "Will it help me to get more money, a nicer home, a better car, more loving relationships?"

Well, it can...but if that is how you define success, fulfillment and true happiness, and if that is all you are seeking through the Law of Attraction, you are selling yourself short. You are at the stage of the Wright brothers and the first airplane. What if attempts to defy the Law of Gravity had stopped there? We would only have a few open-air, rickety light aircraft flying around. Instead others continued to explore the idea of defying the Law of Gravity through flight, building on each new discovery, creating better and better ideas, until bingo, we landed on the moon!

Once you have mastered the Law of Attraction to the skill level where you are attracting the things you want into your life, you become aware of a greater possibility, and of a major change that is already happening within you. It must happen. You cannot help but change. You alter your state of consciousness to higher and higher levels. You BECOME!

The wonderful thing about mastering this law is you realize, if you are to manifest material things into your life, you first hold high level vibrations! Instead of saying, "I will be so happy when I win the lottery, or get that car, or find my soul mate," you come to realize WHEN you become happy and at peace with yourself, you are a perfect match for the things you desire and they come easily and gracefully into existence for you.

It is not the possessions that fulfill you! You feel fulfilled when you are holding an inner calm and sense of abundance. From that center of consciousness, you easily and assuredly bring all the things you desire into your life. The greatest gift of the Law of Attraction is actually revealed in what happens to you in the process of living a life in vibrations of gratitude, wonder, joy, and peace. Then, you do have it all!

3

Observer as creator

If you do not get schwindlig [dizzy] sometimes when you think about these things then you have not really understood it [quantum theory].
– Niels Bohr, world-renowned physicist

The notion the Observer determines reality is the most shocking revelation of quantum physics, and is the underlying mechanism for understanding how the Law of Attraction works. The Observer can choose success, abundance, fulfillment, and true happiness. Everything you are experiencing today is a creation of thoughts and feelings, conscious or unconscious, individual or collective. We get what we expect.

Once confronted with this knowledge of yourself as an energy being, you may be startled into a new way of thinking not only about the things you want in your life but about life's bigger questions: "Who am I? Who are we? Who do I want to be? How can we create a new life story for all of us?" The quest for answers to questions like these is as old as civilization.

Evolution is an on-going process. Creation is still unfolding and we play an important part in defining how the "story" develops. The development of the universe and of humanity is incomplete. Science can now prove the universe is still unfolding and new galaxies are continually being formed. Earth's creation has been unfolding over billions of years. We are not pawns in a play already pre-determined but rather, we are a significant part of on-going creation. We are co-creators contributing our part by selecting and choosing what we expect and thereby, defining the shape and outcome of our personal lives, our communities, and the world we live in. The final chapters of the "story" are not written and completed.

Transform your life and create a new life story as you come to know the power of thoughts and accept thoughts become things. Every thought is a new creation. What have you been thinking? Is there a match with what you have been receiving?

Thoughts arise from the sea of energy moving through consciousness and into creation. We are the only species with this implicate order connection for creation.

Determine what you want — that is your intention. That is the Observer, deciding what you want to experience or create. Then be guided by your intuition on how to achieve it. Intuition is your radar to the actions needed to create whatever you desire. When you learn to act based on intuition you begin to live life completely differently.

Your power is intention! Your intuition is the magic!

Imagine a journey to be enjoyed every step of the way. The journey never stops. It just keeps getting better and better as you keep getting better and better at creating! Realize you are the Observer and Creator. You can use your power to choose your intentions and then, act on intuition to create that reality.

Quantum physics has opened a new era to life's greatest discoveries, uniting science with mysticism, religion, and ancient philosophies. The past 1,000 years have been a time of scientific and technological achievements. The next frontier of man's exploration will be the human mind and consciousness. What mysteries will be solved in the next decades through even greater discoveries in quantum physics as we begin to understand the true power of thoughts, feelings, and our role as conscious creators?

4

Natural law

*So divinely is the world organized that every one of us, in our place
and time, is in balance with everything else.*
– Goethe

There are many natural laws that govern the unfolding of the
universe. They keep our existence predictable by working precisely all the time. Laws like the Law of Cause and Effect, the
Law of Gender, the Law of Polarity, or the Law of Relativity, to
name but a few. We count on them to work in the same way, all
the time.

Dr. Wernher Von Braun, the father of the space program said,

> The natural laws of the universe are so precise that we
> don't have any difficulty building spaceships, sending
> people to the moon, bringing them back safely to earth
> and we can time the landing with the precision of a frac-
> tion of a second.

One important natural law in understanding quantum physics
and the Law of Attraction is the First Law of Thermodynamics.
This law states energy cannot be created or destroyed. That
energy cannot be created, suggests all energy on the planet and
in the universe emerged at the same time. It means we have all
been created from One Source. If energy cannot be destroyed, we
are a huge energy recycling bin constantly moving energy into
form, through form and out of form. Each movement of energy is
a new creation.

I suppose the bruised head of Sir Isaac Newton is another place to start to talk about natural laws. When the apple hit Newton on the head, it got him thinking about stuff that falls, and his curiosity resulted in the formulation of the Law of Gravity. This is a natural law. It did not go through Parliament or debate before it was enacted. But each and every one of us, no matter where we are on the planet, has great respect for this law. You experimented with it from the time you were only a few months old. A wrong move on the sofa did not take you floating into the air. Instead it took you, sometimes painfully but always assuredly, down onto the floor.

We have defied the Law of Gravity by learning to fly. Working within the law to achieve these amazing defying feats did not change the law. Step off a cliff and you assuredly will fall down to the bottom — even though airplanes may be flying overhead! The Law of Gravity is still working as a natural law.

You don't have to think about natural laws for them to work. When you walk, you don't think about the Law of Gravity holding your feet on the ground. Although while you are flying in that airplane, you may be praying what was done to defy the natural law works, at least for the duration of your flight! When you are sitting in a chair, you don't ask the Law of Gravity to hold you down. You just trust and know this natural law works consistently. You can depend on it. So, too, can you depend on the Law of Attraction working all the time — for everyone. You have to learn how to make it work to your advantage just as you learned to trust that you can fly in an airplane — while still respecting it is not a good idea to step off high cliffs!

When you understand the Law of Attraction as a natural predictable law, you can learn to make it work. Unlike the Law of Gravity, you may not be conscious right now of just how the Law of Attraction is working for you — or against you! You can trust and depend on all natural laws. They work consistently all the time, but only by studying them, do you make them work to your advantage.

5

The Law of Attraction

What we send out into our world in the form of a vibration is what is attracted or played back to us. That is the natural law that works with vibrational frequencies coming from our thoughts and feelings. It is the Law of Attraction.

Some people confuse the Law of Attraction with the Law of Polarity and say, "But I thought opposites attract?" Opposites attracting is the Law of Polarity. The Law of Attraction is demonstrated more clearly through the use of a musical tuning fork. It may have been more descriptive to call this the Law of Vibration. When a tuning fork is struck, all similar instruments surrounding the tuning fork soon start to resonate at the same pitch. That is how the Law of Attraction works. Vibrations from thoughts and feelings impact all living things that are then influenced or "entrained" by that vibrational frequency.

There are many wave frequencies in the environment — ultraviolet waves, infrared waves, sound waves, light waves, microwaves, etc. Your body also emits wave frequencies. When you are meditating, your body is typically in alpha- or beta-wave states. Well-trained meditators go into deep delta wavelengths characteristic of a sound sleep — "asleep while awake." In normal sleep patterns, your body cycles through alpha, beta, theta, k-complex, delta, and continuous delta wavelengths. You are constantly in a state of vibration.

Your thoughts and feelings also have a vibration or wave frequency. That vibration aligns you with everything in the universal energy field resonating at the same frequency. You send out a vibration and an identical vibration is attracted or connected back.

In this way the Observer creating reality gives a wonderfully encouraging message. We can choose our vibration by consciously deciding on our feelings. Whatever frequency you are vibrating is what you receive more of. That frequency comes from your feelings. If you think and feel scarcity and fear, the universe responds by producing more of that. If you think and feel anger and hate, you live a life of anger and hate. If you emit a frequency of success and abundance, the universe aligns to give you more of that. The universal energy field does not decide if it is good for you or not, it just matches your vibration.

To experience a new reality, you change your thoughts and feelings. Focus on the good that is happening and what you are grateful for. When you do, your vibration changes and the frequencies around you realign to create what you are now intending. Many factors impact on your ability to hold a high vibration.

Close your eyes and imagine. Last night you went to bed and had a wonderful sleep. You nurtured your body with good food and hydration. Now, you set off to work. The sky is especially blue, the flowers incredibly vivid. You are alert, feeling very much alive. It is a good day. Suddenly a car cuts you off. You ease up on the gas pedal, you relax, and let the anxious driver move into the lane in front of you. The sky is still vividly blue!

Now re-create this image. You stayed out late partying with friends. You overslept and it is going to be a frenetic drive to get to the office on time. Your head aches. You feel dehydrated from the excessive use of alcohol and cigarettes. The greasy burger you had at 2:00 am feels like a lump in your stomach. Suddenly a car cuts you off! Now, the air is blue!

Hhhmmmm....now can you change your thoughts or feelings? Can you express gratitude? Are you in a state of consciousness to remain calm and relaxed?

Your physical body and mind are sensory and response mechanisms through which you experience everything, and through which you affect and create everything. Just as a race car requires exquisite tuning to perform well, care for your physical and mental body are essential to being able to make a choice to vibrate at a consciousness that will attract desirable life experiences.

The encouraging news is who you are now, or who you were yesterday, is not who you need to be in the future. Choose to care for your tuning mechanisms, consciously choose your vibration and you can change your life immediately. Just as the Observer changes the subatomic experience from energy to matter by changing what they expected to see, so too, do you change your reality by changing the way you think and feel. That is the Law of Attraction.

The Law of Attraction in action!

Intentions/Desires – conscious or unconscious

Form thoughts

Thoughts evokes feelings

Feelings have vibrations

Universe responds to the vibrations

You create a new REALITY!

6

Interconnected energy

The energy frequency we send out connects with other similar energy fields and returns amplified! Everything is an energy frequency and all energies mingle and interconnect. Astounding! The classical physics concept that everything was matter and separate, put forward by Sir Isaac Newton in the seventeenth century, has been the accepted wisdom for the past 400 years. Much of what we currently do and the way we think today is based on this construct of matter and separation.

Now our separateness, our state as physical matter, our beliefs and our relationship to the environment and community are being tossed out the window! Newtonian separateness created a world of competition — "I've got to get my share." It created a world of scarcity and isolation.

Quantum physics offers a totally new perspective. There is no shortage of energy and no limit to creation. The entire universe is a sea of energy possibility. There is the potential to create more than enough abundance for all. We only have to choose to make it so. Our interconnectedness makes it possible to take quantum leaps when we draw on this collective energy.

How can we be sure we truly are intertwined energies?

A famous experiment conducted by John Bell, an Irish physicist, tested quantum particle behavior. Bell noticed an unusual thing happening with paired electrons. They rotated in opposite directions and moved at exactly the same speed. When a change in DIRECTION was made to one electron, the other immediately changed direction. When the SPEED of one electron was changed, instantly the speed of the other changed! Bell separated these paired electrons across vast distances and repeated the experiment numerous times. When a change was made to one electron, the other, separated through a significant distance, changed at precisely the same time!

Einstein was baffled by these results. He called it, "spooky action at a distance." For these electrons to communicate, it either meant there was a wavelength moving faster than his discovery of the speed of light or it meant there was no such thing as space. The paired electrons continued to be paired and connected, despite their separation. This discovery made it difficult for Einstein to accept what he was actually seeing in the quantum world.

It meant time and space, as we had known it, did not exist! What it did mean, astoundingly, is everything is connected energetically. Once connected, wavelengths always retain a connection. Have you ever thought about your mother, brother, or friend only to have the phone ring and — guess who is calling! Most of us have had this experience at least once or twice. The term "entanglement" has been used to describe this interconnectivity of all things.

If space does not exist, if all things are interconnected, then what is going on up there in the sky? The idea that space is not an empty void was pursued by English mathematician Paul Dirac. Space, he determined, was a teeming mass of energy with which all energy interacts. It is referred to as the Zero Point Field, so named because at absolute zero, when our present theories say there should be no movement, there continues to be fluctuations in this energy field. The amount of energy happening in space is so great it is estimated to be a factor of ten to the power of 40 — 10 followed by 40 zeros. Physics Professor Richard Feynman remarked, "The energy in a cubic meter of space is enough to boil all the oceans of the world."

Discoveries in quantum physics are challenging everything we believe about ourselves and how we exist on this planet...even empty spaces are a myth! We are a sea of energy.

Ancient Eastern civilizations understood energy flow influenced the human condition. Life force energies were believed to fuel the body. They believed everything in nature and the universe was connected to the power of a Higher Source. Typical approaches to healing explored mental and physical energy blockages as contributing factors to illness, fatigue or loss of life force.

In the West, the body is regarded as a physical structure, a machine, and treated as we treat all machines. If a part is not working, we remove the offending part and replace it with a donor or mechanical part, or we introduce drugs to modify the internal workings. The dominating mechanistic views of the West have the biggest adjustment to make to quantum physics truths. We, in the West, must drastically change our perceptions of many things as we begin to understand the natural laws governing quantum energy. This has implications for science, but it has even greater implications for understanding the human condition, consciousness and our life purpose and meaning.

Seeing ourselves as One, connected through energy, changes everything! Truly it is an amazing time to be alive. Anything is possible! You have the potential to choose to tune into the energy frequency for the life you desire to live!

7

Your success station

You are a sender and receiver of frequencies much like a two-way radio station. If you tune your radio to a light-rock station, you are guaranteed to get light rock music, every time. Move your tuner to heavy metal music, you get heavy metal, every time. You might moan and groan about how much you dislike heavy metal music, but nothing changes until you turn the dial. You get what you tune in to. So it is in your life. You transmit a frequency, and all tuners, all living things, tuned to the same frequency respond to your signal. Your frequency is determining your life experiences and you are choosing which success station you want to be on.

To prove our bodies emitted wavelengths and acted like radio transmitters and receivers, Dr. Gary Schwartz conducted experiments with his students at the University of Arizona. As a child he played with the rabbit ears on his family's black-and-white television, and noticed he could stand between the television and the antennae and make the picture go away. He could also touch the antennae in certain ways and make the picture clearer. It seemed his body was participating in these mysterious wavelengths.

This experience later prompted him to set up a study in which he placed an EEG cap on the head of a bust of Einstein on a table in his office. He passed his hand over the head of the bust. The amplifier crackled, picking up an electromagnetic wave from the movement of his hand. He tried another experiment with a student standing with his left hand over Einstein's head and his right arm extended towards Schwartz, who was seated about three feet away. Schwartz moved his hand again. To their amazement the amplifier again picked up the electromagnetic signal. Some kind of energy signal was passing from Schwartz, through the student, to the antennae.

It seems energy from movement can be detected and measured. The next question is "That might be true for movement energy, but is it true for thought energy? Do our thoughts also have a frequency and can they impact or be picked up by people or things around us?"

Stanford University physicist William Tiller conducted such an experiment to see if thoughts gave off energy and effected a change in the environment. Volunteers held a mental intention to increase the count of randomly generated electrons. A specially-designed device gave out a stream of electrons and recorded the exact number of electrons generated through a counter. More than 1,000 experiments were done in which the rate increased by a significant average of 50,000 electrons. This happened even if the people holding the intention were not in the same room. His obvious conclusion was directed thoughts can alter results even when those thoughts are projected over considerable distance. These research projects and other similar studies resulted in a measurement of the change in energy created by movement and by thought. Thoughts seemed to be having an impact on the operation of the random generator.

We know thoughts trigger feelings. Is it possible the frequency of feelings emanating from thoughts can also impact living things?

Almost inadvertently, Clive Backster discovered a possible impact of feelings on living things. He found when a plant was approached with threatening thoughts, he was actually able to measure a diminishing energy level in the plant. When approached with thoughts of love, the opposite occurred.

He stumbled across this realization as he was watering a plant in his office. Backster is a leading lie-detector expert in the US. As he watered the plant the idea came to him to use his lie-detector equipment to measure how long it takes for water to go up into the leaves. His expectation was he would see an immediate upward trend in the ink tracing but the opposite happened. The dip or downward trend that actually happened is what he would expect to get with a person if they were experiencing fear of detection. He decided to test further to see if it could indeed be a fear response. He dipped the leaf into a cup of coffee. That did not cause a threat or result in a similar downward trend on the graph. Then he thought about getting a match and burning the leaf.

At the very moment he had the thought, the recording nearly went off the polygraph chart! He had not burned the plant. He only thought about doing it! It seemed the plant picked up energy from him akin to reading his thoughts.

Our physical movements, thoughts, and emotions all generate a vibration that can have an impact on all living things. What implication does that have for you? The answer is fundamental to the Law of Attraction. You have a thought. The thought creates a feeling. The feeling has a vibration. Whatever vibration you send out impacts on other living things and shapes your experience. You are creating through the resonance of your vibrations.

The exciting news is the frequency you are currently tuned in to is not where you have to stay. If you are unhappy with any aspect of your life, you can change your frequency (feelings) about that aspect of your life and align with different results!

Have you ever awakened experiencing a wonderful day and realized everyone around you also seems to be having a great day? An interesting coincidence? Or you may start your day in a great mood and walk into a room of unhappy, depressed people. Suddenly, your energy shifts. Your mood changes even without having a conversation with them as you allow yourself to fall prey to the energies they are emitting! Or perhaps you get on a subway, and for some unknown reason, you feel your happy feeling slipping away. You are not sure why.

You are influenced by your own energies, but you are also entrained and resonating to the energies of the people around you. The challenge to conscious attraction is to hold fast to the energy you want to bring into your life in the face of negative influences.

Every thought, feeling and movement we make is being experienced by the people around us. Consider how important it is then, to choose your friends and your environment very carefully. Each interaction is shaping your life. Can you imagine your life resonating success in a fulfilling work environment, a contented home life, joyful and happy social relations, and a deep inner spiritual peace? This life awaits you! Adjust your dial accordingly!

8

"I will be happy — when ...?"

A client I was coaching told me how excited she was when a mortgage calculation showed she could have her home paid for in seven years. Then she immediately focused on what she would need to do to make that happen. The shift in thinking to how to make this happen suddenly switched her emotion from excitement to one of stress and anxiety. She tuned into a different station!

Keeping a vibration of the way we would feel as though what we want has already happened is essential to attracting success. It is from a positive emotional place that quantum abundant solutions are brought to us. If my client continues to hold feelings of stress wondering how to meet her monthly payments, she may never attract the abundance she could if she remained in the full-grin, happy feeling she experienced when she thought about her house totally paid for. As odd as it may seem, you have to feel as though you are already in possession of what you want before it manifests. By holding the feeling, the Law of Attraction aligns with that vibration and brings more of the same to you.

Let's use a sports example, something more familiar. Athletes know this stuff. They might not call it the Law of Attraction, but they know when the team and the crowd are "up," they give their peak performance, and when the team and the crowd are "down," they do not ... almost every time.

If athletes want to win Olympic gold, they don't focus on all the times they have failed, the moves they cannot do well, the falls they have taken or the competitions they didn't win. If you heard an athlete talking this way, you could predict right away he or she would not likely be standing on the podium. Instead the gold medalist is the athlete who puts the failed performances behind them, focuses on the thrill of achieving excellence, and holds an emotional vibration of the winning performance as though it has already happened.

The idea you will "be happy when" is all backwards. If you work on the BEING, if you work on your inside happiness and joy, you are astounded by the speed at which things materialize in your life to support that happy feeling.

The true secret to the Law of Attraction is feeling happy, at peace and calm regardless of your external environment. You come to realize true happiness does not come from the external things. These external things contribute to our happiness only if we already hold an emotion of well-being and success.

If you choose to live your life in a high vibration, anticipating riches being attracted to you, in the whole scheme of things, what does it mean? Regardless of the external abundance you may or may not acquire, it means you are living a life resonating success. You are living a life feeling fulfilled and happy. Perhaps you know people who have lots of things but who experience little happiness. Wouldn't you agree that true abundance lies primarily in your feelings?

In the later three segments of the book, you are provided with a "how-to" guide to the Law of Attraction. At this point in our discussion of "Why is the Law of Attraction a law?" is a brief introduction to the Soul Abundant three step method — BE – HAVE – DO — to verify these Law of Attraction skills can be learned.

It is a simple method to remember, but don't be fooled into expecting to master it in one day! It is a life-long process — a new way of BEING.

9

"To DO is to BE"

All that we are is a result of what we have thought.
– Buddha

The Law of Attraction is mastered by acquiring specific skills. There are different ways to describe the techniques to create through attraction. The Soul Abundant approach involves three distinct steps referred to as the BE – HAVE – DO method.

In the West, we believe success is related to what we do. We do not expect to find success through inner quietude. For us, it is all about busi-ness. Our sequence is the exact opposite. It is DO – HAVE – BE! When we have a problem, we ask, "What do we need to do?" We immediately want to take action to solve the problem.

If we desire higher levels of income, we think, "What can I DO to make more money?" We believe if we DO enough, we will HAVE all the things we desire and then we will BE the person we would like to be. It goes like this, "I have to do three jobs right now, to have enough money to buy the house I want. When I get the house I will be so happy." OR "I have to win a lottery (that's what I need to do), to have enough money, so that I can be really happy."

Doing is something happening outside of us. It does not connect our feelings to success. It just says if you work hard enough you can get anything you desire. It does not start with an alignment of character, values, or ethics.

Quantum physics says it is first about our Being. It is about our emotional vibration. We first be-come the person we were intended to be, then we have a vibration in alignment with our dreams, and only then can we tap into the intuitive genius of the universe to do the inspired, intuitive actions.

Success is an inside job. Success through the Law of Attraction in this three-step process begins with personal growth and intention.

> BE. *Clarity of INTENTION*
> HAVE. *An alignment of FEELINGS/CONSCIOUSNESS*
> DO. *Inspired (in spirit) INTUITIVE action*

Dr. Fred Alan Wolfe, in his book Taking the Quantum Leap, says, "To BE or NOT to BE is not the Question — it is the Answer!"

You are as powerful through your BEING as you can IMAGINE!

You enter into a process to become the person you were intended to be by tapping into your soul or inner voice. That is how you BE-come. You are clear about the success you desire. It can mean being clear about the job or the relationship you want, or it can be getting clear about your values and life purpose. Whatever it is you dream, hold fast to the thought of your intention. You may be living in poverty but you hold a thought of how affluent you envision yourself to be. You may want to build the house of your dreams, or meet your soul mate. Although you may be living in very humble dwellings or feeling very lonely, you hold the thought with absolute certainty what you intend is about to appear. I know it sounds strange, but that is the way it works. It is the secret successful people have known all along.

My husband and I wanted to rent a furnished home in Kingston, Ontario. I surfed the Internet without success. I was doing what many of us do when we want something in our lives. We are not really sure what we want so we just go window shopping, hoping something will show up. I realized I was not clear about where I wanted to live, how long I wanted to be there or what the house would look like. After some reflection, I decided I wanted something relatively small but tastefully appointed, right in the inner city of Kingston. It would be bright and well suited to doing my writing. I wanted to rent for five months. It would have the right "feeling" for the creative journey I was about to embark upon. Within days of getting clarity, I did another Internet search. This time a new site came up. There it was! A house rental offered for the exact timeframes. It met all my criteria! Intriguingly, the owner was a writer who worked from home and was now going on assignment for five months! The house was filled with creative writing energy! Not only did it meet my creative needs but it also was the connection that attracted me to my publisher!

Once you are clear about what you intend, hold a high vibration of expectation and belief. This is the HAVE step of the process. You hold a feeling in alignment with what you want. It is devoid of uncertainty, fear, doubt, or any low level emotional vibrations. It is the vibration of emotion or feelings that determine the resonance of what is being attracted. You may be wanting to meet your soul mate, but if you are holding a vibration of skepticism and doubt, you attract experiences to reinforce failure.

The third and last step is DO — Inspired INTUITIVE actions. These are rich and abundant ideas to bring your dreams to reality. Inspired actions are in contrast to the linear solutions of most goal setting and action planning models, but are the model of great discoveries and creativity.

Before we move into the techniques to help you become a master of the Law of Attraction, let's briefly investigate ancient Mayan and Hopi prophecies and astrology to understand if they hold any explanation for the current global interest in this law. You will also discover the origins of duality, the divisive attitude responsible for discontent and scarcity thinking on the planet today. It is the biggest challenge faced in successfully applying the law. Release attitudes of dualism and you move into a new realm of consciousness, a realm of non-duality. You move into the realm where success and abundance can be attracted.

All this may seem mysterious and complex. It will soon become clearer. Take the time to immerse yourself in the ideas. The greatest gift of the Law of Attraction is what happens to you in the process of living a life in vibrations of gratitude, acceptance, joy, love, and peace.

> Your First Insight: We are interconnected energy with the power to create our world through our thoughts and feelings.

Getting started

Personal change involves becoming informed, then integrating the new ideas and behaviors into your daily routine, and finally, internalizing them, so they are who you BECOME. It is all about you BEING MORE!

Start this week by holding a positive intention to attract a parking space close to the door — or far away, if walking is one of your New Year's resolutions! See how it manifests for you!

Hold a happy vibration for one entire day. See how quickly you can shift your focus to what there is to celebrate about a situation when something negative happens. Write down your experiences.

Begin a Gratitude journal. Gratitude is the turning point to progressively higher consciousness. Begin each day with gratitude, taking a few minutes to write down all you are grateful for in your life at that moment.

Pay special attention to your physical and mental well-being for several days, getting ample rest, hydration, nourishment and exercise. Note the impact this has on your ability to hold higher levels of vibration or consciousness.

Summary

Why is the Law of Attraction a law?

The universe is governed by natural laws consistently operating in the same precise ways.

You are a quantum energy being. Everything in the universe is energy.

Quantum physics teaches us the Observer creates the reality. You create your reality.

The First Law of Thermodynamics is energy cannot be created or destroyed.

We are all interconnected, having originated from one energy Source.

Like a tuning fork, whatever frequency you vibrate causes all things around you to resonate at the same frequency.

You bring into your life whatever you are vibrating, either positive or negative.

Energy is constantly moving into form, through form, and out of form.

A thought evokes a feeling, the feeling has a vibration, and the universe responds to that vibration.

The Law of Attraction is a natural law that works the same way for everyone all the time.

The Law of Attraction shows us the importance of raising our consciousness and connecting as One with the planet.

Prophecies and duality

In its primordial condition, humankind had possessed an instinctive knowledge of the profound sacred unity and interconnectedness of the world but under the influence of the Western mind, especially its modern expression, the course of history brought about a deep schism between humankind and nature, and a desacralization of the world.
– Richard Tarnas, Cosmos and Psyche

10

Amazing discoveries yet to come?

What appears to be a stable, tangible, visible, audible world is an illusion. It is dynamic and kaleidoscopic — not really "there." What we normally see is the explicit or unfolded order of things rather like watching a movie. But there is an underlying order that is mother and father to the second-generation reality — the implicate or enfolded.
    – Physicist David Bohm

In "Prophecies and duality," we seek to decode the wisdom and mysteries of the Mayan and Hopi prophecies and examine some astonishing astrological findings. Also in this segment, we explore an important concept called duality. This dualistic mindset holds us back from attaining the personal success and the benevolent society to which we aspire.

Is there anything in these prophecies we can learn to help us understand and apply the Law of Attraction? Are there insights as to why the Law of Attraction has gained such rapid popularity when the ideas have been known for thousands of years?

When I first started teaching the Attracting Success seminars, I was intrigued by a study reported by Dr. Valerie Hunt in her book, *Infinite Mind*. It was a story linked to the Mayan calendar:

The source of this story reported by Valerie Hunt is from Robert Anton Wilson's book, *Cosmic Trigger*. A group of computer scien-

tists from Stanford University, intrigued by the speed of technological development, decided to plot the great discoveries in the
world, starting from about 4,000 or 5,000 B.C.E. to modern civilization.

This included things such as the discovery of the wheel, the
printing press, the steam engine, up to the splitting of the atom,
and the advent of computers.

Their results created a hyperbolic curve, flattening out around
1975. With this historic perspective, they were intrigued by the
possibility of projecting the pattern to predict future discoveries.
These computer experts were startled when the graph shot off
the paper with an upwards sweep in the year 2011 recording 18
discoveries each equal in impact to the splitting of the atom and
all happening in the last part of the year 2010.

At this point one of the scientists proposed a connection to the
Mayan calendar with its projections for the completion of the
Ninth and last great cycle of evolution occurring in the year
2011, marking the arrival of highest consciousness of man as a
co-creator of his universe.

This little experiment may challenge what seems to be a fairly
common thought — everything that is to be known is already
known and all the truly great discoveries have already been
made. Could we instead be in for our most exciting discoveries in
the future? Perhaps the Mayan calendar holds clues as to what
those discoveries might be.

After I read this story in Dr. Hunt's book, the Mayan and Hopi
prophecies kept coming up in my life, in bookstores and in conversation. The last step in the Soul Abundant method of applying the Law of Attraction is the importance of trusting your intu-

ition. I finally decided to listen to mine! It was time for me to become familiar with the prophecies.

I now understand why I needed to include this in our journey to greater inner peace and abundance. These prophecies provide a map for evolution to our higher consciousness. They are not a vague projection of potential physical events. They are intriguing. Many of the prophecies make it crystal clear there is a destiny, a time of awakening, and it is happening right now! Understanding the Law of Attraction and learning how to consciously apply this law is part of a prophesized evolution. The attention being paid to the Law of Attraction is unfolding from the implicate order exactly in accordance with prophecy.

The "implicate or the enfolded" is constantly being revealed and quantum physics explains our role in the unfolding of the implicit to the explicit through the power of our thoughts.

11

Evolution prophecies

The story told by the Mayan Calendar scholars may or may not be precise, but its forecasts do hold some intriguing parallels to what unfolded in the past and what seems to be unfolding today. You may even have been attracted to explore the Law of Attraction because you are in tune with the prophecies of the Mayan calendar!

The Mayan Calendar uses an intriguing mathematical formula dating the planet back 16 billion years to the beginning of time, and projecting forward to the completion of this evolutionary cycle in 2011. This forecast does not suggest life ceases to exist on that date. It implies the process for the full evolution of humans began 16 billion years ago and is soon coming to the close of one of its Nine Great Cycles. If we exercise our free will and make appropriate choices, we are poised with the potential to become the evolved, loving creatures we were intended to be! We are a unique species able to choose our thoughts and actions. Our choices determine our outcomes.

We in the western hemisphere are literal and scientific in our thinking. If the idea of paying attention to the prophecies from ancient documents is making you a little skeptical, dubious, or nervous, it is not surprising. You have been taught to be left-brained and analytical, as have I! What opened my mind and made me explore these ideas is the number of Western scientific thinkers now embracing and researching the concepts. The science supporting what the ancients knew thousands of years ago is growing. Once again, science, spirituality, and metaphysics are all singing the same song. This way of thinking requires greater use of our right-brain hemispheres, our intuitive, creative thought processes, and finding a balance between left and right brain hemispheres.

In each of us, the separation of left brain (analytical side) and right brain (creative, intuitive side) parallels the global worldview separation of East and West. As our individual minds need to become balanced, so too, do the East and West splits on our planet need to seek a power balance. We are being called upon to initiate a return to the center, balancing world power, and balancing an evolved mind. The Mayan Calendar holds some fascinating insights for this balancing process and forecasts specific dates for this to happen in the not-too-distant future.

A few years ago, my husband and I were invited to attend a leadership conference in Cancun, Mexico. We stopped at an information booth at the airport to get directions to our resort and ended up getting a sales pitch to attend a time-share presentation. Normally we avoid these presentations, but this one had features that intrigued us. It offered a tour of the resort before our event started, but more exciting, it included a tour of the Mayan ruins at Chichen Itza.

We climbed the Pyramid of Kukulcan, March 23, two days after the spring equinox. We were in awe of the mathematical and astrological genius of the ancient Mayans. How could they have possessed such advanced knowledge and skills thousands of years ago? Many of the ruins at Chichen Itza are meticulously constructed to allow light patterns to reflect in particular directions at precise astrological times. At the Pyramid of Kukulcan, during the spring and autumn equinox, you see a shadow appearing like a serpent weaving either up or down the steep

stairs to the top of the pyramid. The serpent alternates directions on each of the equinoxes and is visible around those days
only. The uniqueness of the serpent, with its seven light scales
and six dark scales creating a wavelike pattern is the perception
the serpent is actually moving.

This structure represents the Mayan belief there are 13 heavens,
each made up of seven days and six nights, consistent with the
Christian belief of the earth being created in seven days and six
nights. But these days are not the 24-hour clock modern civilization has created to understand time. A Mayan Day in the
prophecies can mean millions of our modern years and the
length of a day varies within each of the evolutionary Great
Cycles. There are nine levels of the pyramid representing the
nine Great Cycles of evolution required to reach the final creation. An interesting parallel to the months required for human
gestation!

Volumes of books written by the Mayans were destroyed by the
conquering Spaniards. Only three of the volumes survived. It is
from these volumes and the artifacts of carved calendars that the
divine evolutionary plan held by the Mayans is being pieced
together and revealed today. The interpretations bear some similarity to stories in Revelations and Genesis! Ironically, what the
Spanish priests sought to eradicate when they burned the
Mayan books to make way for Christianity actually contained
teachings very similar to Biblical messages!

I've chosen highlights from the Mayan prophecies to get you
thinking about the Law of Attraction in a new context. You benefit from understanding the Law of Attraction as part of the total
cosmic plan and not just as a way to get you more things you
want. Accepting the notion of a cosmic intention requires right-
brain thinking. That is thinking done in faith and from intuition.

Does this intrigue you? Learn to trust your intuition and feelings to formulate original thoughts and opinions. Stay open to possibility!

12

Higher consciousness

We all pay attention to calendars. Most ancient cultures had calendars with specific messages about the days and seasons of the year but their calendars also held spiritual information about their relationship with God and the cosmos.

One of the best sources of information on the Mayan calendar is Dr. Carl Johan Calleman, author of *The Mayan Calendar and the Transformation of Consciousness*. He holds a Ph.D. in physical biology. Calleman began his studies on the Mayan Calendar in 1979 as a hobby and is now a leading expert on the subject. He does not interpret the calendar as a projection of physical events or happenings but rather he interprets the spiritual calendars of the Mayans as a metaphysical map for today's evolution of human consciousness. His work has been used as the primary source of data for our exploration in this section. Whether he is exact in his interpretations and dates, we can only wait and see. Certainly, the historical fit is compelling.

The Mayan Calendars were not just physical calendars designed to reflect our cycle around the sun, as is the Gregorian calendar we currently use throughout the world (introduced by Pope Gregory back in 1582). They were also spiritual calendars. Spiritual calendars hold wisdoms beyond knowing what day or earths orbit we are in. With our modern day emphasis on the Gregorian calendar, ancient spiritual calendars were lost, hidden, or discouraged from use. Our Gregorian calendar serves one purpose only, to track and record our physical relationship to the 365?-day cycle around the sun.

The Mayans had three calendars. They were aware of the earth's physical rotation around the sun, but this 365-day calendar was used only for paying taxes and observing agricultural cycles. It was called the HAAB Calendar. Their second calendar was a personal and astrological calendar called the TZOLK'IN. It had 260 days and was used to determine your name at birth and your personal life plan. A third Divine or Prophetic calendar called the TUN operated on a 360-day cycle. It was used to predict a path of consciousness and prophecy. The personal (TZOLK'IN) and the divine (TUN) calendars worked together like two cogged and interlocking wheels.

The spiritual calendars respected the belief that thought starts from a divine place. It starts with Source energy or consciousness moving through light and connecting with the individual through thought, ultimately, manifesting into form. Predicting this light energy connection to the individual was the role of the TUN calendar. It was the predictor of the greater consciousness where everything emanates and where thought originates.

The TZOLK'IN personal calendar explained your life purpose. You knew why you came here and what you were meant to learn. The first part of the name given to you was the name of the day you were born. That day had a specific meaning and purpose. You choose to be born on that day for a reason and you were here to fulfill that reason. You and everyone else in the civilization knew your life purpose just by hearing your name.

Our Gregorian calendar leaves us without any awareness of why we are here or who we are. Our calendar tells us nothing about ourselves. It only tells us where we are in relation to the sun. Many of us in Western society have at least a passing interest in horoscopes because it is here we are linked to one type of ancient spiritual calendar with life purpose messages.

It is difficult enough when others don't know who we are! But when we struggle to understand "Who am I?" and "Why am I here?" we feel isolated, lost, and stressed. We see evidence of this all around us. Think in particular about the numerous horrific incidents of young people killing each other in what should be their haven of camaraderie — their schools. This seems to be a very loud collective consciousness cry for inclusion, acceptance, purpose, and meaning.

Would you like to know what some of the ancient spiritual calendars can tell you about who you are and why you are here?

13

Nine Great Cycles

Before we can address those questions, let's take a few minutes to understand how these calendars work and why they might be able to give us profound insights. The HAAB calendar is akin to our Gregorian calendar. We have no difficulty tracking the physical changes our proximity and orbit around the sun provide, but we lack a spiritual calendar, and that is why looking at the TZOLK'IN and TUN calendars can give us information to which we normally do not have access.

Using the mathematical formulas based on the 13 heavens and nine Great Cycles from the TZOLK'IN and the TUN calendars, we can track some historic events from the cosmic plan. We can draw our own conclusions about the accuracy of the calendars for predicting the future based on their success in predicting the past. Is it possible that looking at future projections may answer some of our questions about who we are and our reasons for being here at this time?

There are nine Great Cycles of evolution described in the calendar. Each cycle has its unique purpose in the evolutionary process. As we briefly describe each of the nine cycles, it is noteworthy that the middle, or the fifth day, of each of the cycles is the turning point or "budding point," as it was called by the Mayans. That is the point at which the first breakthroughs or trends of what will become for the cycle begin to emerge. The major events of the fifth day provide insights to the new cycle, a clash point between the letting go of the old cycle which may be struggling to hang on, and the essence of the new beginning to emerge.

Another significant milestone of each cycle is the seventh day. That is the end of the cycle and the point at which huge break-throughs occur — what we call quantum leaps. As we describe each of the nine cycles, these are the two most important aspects to watch for to understand the process that is emerging. Notice also the similarity to the biblical references to creation, which was purported to have occurred in six nights and seven days: "And on the seventh day the Lord rested." In the Mayan calendar on the seventh day, all the vestiges of the old cycle have been lost and the total intent of the new cycle is freely being created. On the seventh day, we see great changes. Remember, the term day is not the 24-hour clock. It refers to the heavens of creation and the duration of those days depends on the speed of evolution of the particular cycle. Each cycle has a different duration getting shorter and shorter as it comes closer to the ninth and final cycle. Let's take a 16-billion-year stroll through these Great Cycles!

The First Great Cycle is called the Cellular Cycle and took between 15 and 16 billion years to complete. On the seventh day of this cycle, which lasted for 1.26 billon years, we see the emergence of the first live cells. This was a period of evolution characterized by action and reaction.

The Second Great Cycle is the Mammalian Cycle. It lasted for 820 million years. The seventh day of this cycle took 63 million years. On the seventh day was an evolution from sea to land, from fish to birds. The development of a brain was part of this phase. With a brain, the level of functioning has increased to one of stimulus and response.

The Third Great Cycle is the Familial Cycle. It took 41 million years to move through the 13 heavens of seven days and six nights. The seventh day, which lasted 3.2 million years, is marked by the arrival of bipedal apes. There is an increased sophistication from stimulus response to stimulus and individual response and a shift from herd to individual.

The Fourth Great Cycle is the Tribal Cycle, which started 2.2 million years ago. On the seventh day we see the first arrival of Homo sapiens. This seventh day lasted for 160,000 years. This period is characterized by the development of mind. In this great cycle is the discovery of fire and the occurrence of the Ice Age.

The Fifth Great Cycle, called the Regional Cycle, occurred in 102,000 B.C.E and is the beginning of the Age of Reason and the basis of culture. We see the first efforts of agriculture at the end of the cycle on the seventh day, which lasted 7,900 years. In this cycle there is the emergence of both culture and art.

The Sixth Great Cycle is the National Cycle, a time of great breakthrough. In this cycle, around 3,115 B.C.E., Egypt becomes the first nation on earth. Writing is developed. Moses brings down the first laws. The beginning of this cycle is also symbolized by the story of the casting out of Adam and Eve from the Garden of Eden. That expulsion results in a totally new thought process: dualism. This separateness — individuals from God, right from wrong, good from evil, individuals and nature — has plagued humanity since this time. In this cycle we see the appearance of Christianity as well as the Dark Ages. On the seventh day, which lasted 3,940 years, science and capitalism emerge.

The Seventh Great Cycle is the Planetary Cycle, the beginning of modern civilization and the start of the Industrial Revolution.

This is the time of Sir Isaac Newton and classical physics that further separates man from his universe, thereby creating an even
stronger sense of dualism. It is the time of René Descartes, who
further separated body and mind; of Copernicus and Darwin, who
minimized the relevance of man inside his universe. It is a Cycle
of Power — power in machines and power in politics and corporations. The last day, or seventh day of this cycle, ended on January
4, 1999. The expanded access to the Internet marked a whole new
shift in power and control into the hands of the meek. Almost
everyone has equal access to all information. It is no longer possible to rule by fear, secrecy, and power.

This cycle solidified the idea of dualism. We experienced two
world wars and we saw the advent of automation and technology in this cycle. The seventh day, which lasted 19.7 years, was
characterized by the discovery of the Internet. On January 5,
1999, we entered...

The Eighth Great Cycle, the Galactic Cycle. This cycle is characterized by ethics and spirituality. One of the significant events at
the beginning of this cycle was Y2K. At this time, a great many
of us worried about what would happen when all the power
structures of the world lost access to the Internet. It showed how
weak our political, corporate, and economic systems could poten-
tially be! Already in this cycle, we are expanding our awareness
of our universe, of quantum physics and concepts like the Law of
Attraction. We experience ourselves as energy, coming to terms
with our connection to One Source energy field.

In this cycle, time is speeding up. Where it took the Cellular
Cycle 16 billion years to move through the 13 Heavens of creation (seven days and six nights), this cycle of creation will be
completed in a mere 12.8 years. In your lifetime, you will live
through three Great Cycles. Never in the history of the planet

has that occurred. It is no wonder it feels like we are living in amazing times! It is no wonder we feel time is moving too quickly. This cycle will be completed by February 9, 2011. The seventh day of this cycle will last only 360 days. We can anticipate amazing discoveries. Perhaps that is what the Stanford University computer programmers noted on their technological discoveries experiment.

At that time, we move into the last cycle of creation and this nine cycle phase of evolution will be completed according to the Mayans.

The Ninth and last Great Cycle is the Universal Cycle. It will take only 260 days to complete. This ninth and last Great Cycle starts on February 10, 2011, and ends on October 28, 2011. The seventh day will be only 20 days long. Humanity will achieve the highest level of consciousness fulfilling the fundamental spiritual promise of a heaven on earth.

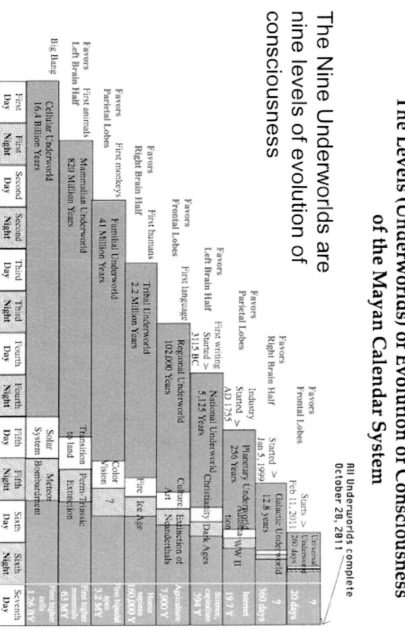

The Levels (Underworlds) of Evolution of Consciousness
of the Mayan Calendar System

The Nine Underworlds are nine levels of evolution of consciousness

14

Is this truth?

Is there truth to the Mayan prophecy? Are these dates accurate? Is it possible to predict the future?

You decide.

This brief historical study, from the excellent work of Dr. Calleman, has revealed some intriguing accuracies in past projections. For those who are skeptical, you won't have long to wait to determine its future accuracy. But does it really matter if the calendar is precise in its predictions? What is the worst that could happen? If you choose to believe this Mayan cosmic plan has some basis in truth and you decide to live your life and act accordingly, you choose to live in the Eighth Great Cycle of Ethics and Spirituality. You live without judgment of others. You choose to uphold an attitude of joy, peace, and love realizing, as the Mayans say in greeting, "Lak ech" — "I am another you." You become conscious we are all One and you choose to participate in the global movement towards higher ethics, spirituality, and more enlightened consciousness. In all, you contribute to a greater good.

If you live your life in this way, will it matter whether the prophecy is fulfilled in the timeframes predicted? Will it matter whether they have been interpreted accurately? If you choose to take heed of what they are suggesting we need to do right now, you choose to act in faith and trust knowing a better world is possible if we only chose it to be so. You will have gained your own heaven on earth!

According to the Mayan calendar the last Great Cycle, the one we have just passed through that ended on January 4, 1999, the Planetary Cycle, was about power. Power for the past 400 years has resided predominately in the Western hemisphere. This next cycle of evolution is one of ethics and spirituality. Are our actions at all times ethical? Do we seek success and true happiness in a consciousness of ethics, spirituality and higher purpose?

This shift away from control and power is referenced also in an ancient Hopi prophecy, *The Hopi Survival Kit: The Prophecies, Instructions and Warnings Revealed by the Last Elders* written by Thomas E. Mails:

The Hopi elders say,

> The time will come when common people will become concerned and frustrated because they can no longer live in a hectic world. They will be against the bloodthirsty policies and deceitfulness of world leaders. The unrest will be worldwide as they foresee the hope of living in peace has become hopeless. The common man will band together to fight for world peace. They realize their leaders have failed. The last battle will be between good and evil. Cleanse the heart of the people and restore our Mother Earth from illness and the wicked will be gotten rid of.

What Hopi legend describes is similar to the Mayan interpretation of where we are right now in the declining power dominance of the Planetary Cycle in 1999. We are midway through the Galactic Cycle. There is a period of letting go. It is the release of power-based attitudes and methods that have to be abandoned for the new Cycle of Ethics and Spirituality to unfold. The fifth day of the Galactic Cycle spans from mid-November, 2006, to mid-November, 2007. You recall it is on the fifth day of each new cycle we see the essence of the last cycle struggling to stay in control. This will be experienced as the last throes of the power elite grasp at any means to maintain their power base.

Observe this behavior in our corporations and political systems. There is rapidly growing disenchantment with the power-based leaders who show signs of corruption, bloat, and loss of ethics.

The middle of the cycle is also the budding point, the time at which signs of the essence of the cycle begin to be revealed. On this, the fifth day of our Cycle of Ethics and Spirituality, are we already experiencing signs of what lies ahead?

It is intriguing the DVD *The Secret,* based on the concepts of the Law of Attraction, broke many previous records for book and DVD sales in a one month period in December, 2006. Sales continue to break records without any paid advertising. Is this the essence of what is to come in the Galactic Cycle? Is this the budding of the new spirituality? Is this success happening because at a deeper level of knowing we see in this information and the Law of Attraction the tools to live in a world of higher consciousness?

All this material on prophecies and consciousness has been available in bookstores and offered in seminars for years; however, it has suddenly spilled over into the mainstream culture. People who would never before have considered wandering into a new age or self-help section of a bookstore are now showing interest...by divine design perhaps? As Swami Beyondananda says, "The time has come for those who have been seeking inner peace to let it spill out into the world!"

Dr. Calleman's theory describes some of what we can expect to see as symptoms of making this transition between Great Cycles, especially having to make three Great Cycle transitions in our lifetime! It is a wake-up call for those who resist the natural wave of evolution. Resistance to any evolutionary process generates great stress, often severe enough that those of the species who do not adapt are lost.

He expounds on what many are experiencing as these transitions unfold in an excerpt from his book, *The Mayan Calendar and the Transformation of Consciousness*:

> Burnout is a sign that many people (subconsciously) desire to transcend the consciousness of the Planetary Cycle. Our bodies are telling us we are not aligned with the divine plan and are refusing to go on. This should be a wake up call.

> The burnout phenomenon has increased dramatically in many countries where people are victimized by stress, seemingly because of the high pace of work around them. In reality, burnout is a result of the increasingly more pronounced conflicts between consciousness generated by the Planetary Cycles and that being created by the newly emerging more spiritual Galactic Cycles. As a result, the symptoms are becoming more serious. The only true remedy is to align our lives with the cosmic evolution toward enlightenment and to focus our whole existence, thinking, acting and being — there is no turning around.

It took 16.4 billion years to create the first cell in the first Great Cycle. The first two cycles took 17 billion years to complete! Now, the last two Great Cycles will happen in a total of about 14 years! Both the Hopi and Mayan prophecies talk about a speeding up of time, and I am sure all of us agree we have had that feeling. The mathematical formulas of the Mayan calendar graphically portray why you feel that way. We are the first people to live through three Great Cycles in one lifetime! That is a lot of change from our cultural upbringing in a cycle embracing power and duality to shift to ethics and spirituality and, finally, to highest consciousness.

We are now in the midst of the struggle to let go of the Planetary Cycle, dominated by rational mind, ego, and power, and are being called upon to move to the next stage of evolution, the Galactic Cycle of ethics and spirit. We need to release ourselves from the powers of our rational mind and ego to successfully make this crossing. When you cease nurturing and glorifying ego, a tremendous surge of energy and freedom emerges that you can direct toward the greater good.

When the process of evolution was slower, we would never have had to make this amount of change in one lifetime. Now the need for change from a power-centered worldview to a worldview of ethics and spirituality is rapidly upon us.

We have taken a brief look at the Mayan and Hopi prophecies telling us the time for change from a power-based society to one of ethics and spirituality is now. There are some other spiritual calendars still available to us. What about astrology? Are there spiritual messages in the stars — as there were 2,000 years ago?

15

It's in the stars

The signs in the sky were indicators of a paradigm shift, much as we are today transitioning into the New Age of Aquarius. On Thanksgiving Day, November 23, 2006, the King Planet Jupiter moved into its home sign of Sagittarius. From December 8–10th and again on December 17–19th, a rare stellium of six planets, including Jupiter and Pluto, formed in the sign of the archer. Sagittarius rules religion and philosophy. Are the stars harbingers of a new spiritual renaissance on the horizon? As we move cautiously forward into a future of uncertain yet unlimited potential, we can only wonder.

The above is an excerpt from an article by Judith Goldberg, a karmic astrologer writing about her investigation into the actual birth date of Jesus.

There are some interesting coincidences here consistent with the mid-November, 2006, Mayan dates of the fifth day of the Galactic Cycle. It appears as though there are many references to this Cycle of Ethics and Spirituality emerging from different sources. Notice some of the similarities between the ancient Hopi message and current astrologers:

In the Hopi prophecies, it is written:

One day certain stars will come together in a row as happened thousands of years ago. It is a time of purifying the land. It has been said that this event will bring about one of two things, destruction or the prosperity to renew earth to its original wholesomeness.

And here is what astrologer Phil Booth has to say about 2007:

Pluto and Jupiter will travel at the Galactic center of our universe all through 2007. This is a momentous time of great intensity and change that has probably not been seen for 2,000 years. There is a hint of something about to be born. Perhaps it is a new global understanding of who we are, whence we came and where we are going. Perhaps, indeed, we are in the early stages of the emergence of a new religious belief system.

These unusual planetary alignments, described by Goldberg, Booth, and the Hopi legends, all speak of a spiritual awakening and of a stellar configuration not seen since the time of the birth of Christ, and are consistent with the timing and messages of the Mayan calendars.

Giving credence to spiritual messages or to astrology is pooh-poohed in most Western cultures. You may question how any of this has relevance to attaining the success you desire. Some of the world's wealthiest may not agree with your reluctance to seek guidance through spiritual messages. Here is an opinion on spiritual guidance from Aristotle Onassis, one of the world's richest men:

Certainly one does not need an astrologist to become a millionaire. Then he quickly added that, to become a billionaire, it is essential!

It seems many highly successful people have relied upon messages from spiritual calendars to guide their decision-making. If there is to be an emergence of a new world spiritual understanding, all the things we study in the Law of Attraction provide us with the skills we need to embrace this shift to a new world order. We trust in a higher order of the universe, experience ourselves as interconnected, let go of our egos and dualistic nature, and concentrate on the best each and every individual has to offer. In so doing, we fulfill a great plan and pave the way for a new world vision to emerge...and we begin to gain full mastery of the natural Law of Attraction.

16

Signs confirming change

The Mayan Calendar hints of a future of phenomenal change. How, literally, we interpret or accept the teachings of the calendar is a personal choice. Whether or not you accept the projections of the Mayan Calendar or other prophetic calendars, you will be intrigued by how the skills to apply the Law of Attraction are in alignment with the skills necessary to shift from a Great Cycle that embraced power and ego, to one free of dualism, embracing ethics and spirituality.

Look for the signs around us that support the Mayan Calendar prophecies:

We are in the midst of a huge power/ethics struggle in business, politics, and community.

We know there are significantly more people experiencing a stressed lifestyle and experiencing burnout than we would have seen 50 years ago.

We have all experienced the sensation that things seem to be speeding up.

There is great dissatisfaction with politics and policies that marginalize and alienate individuals and nations.

Corporations are showing signs of bloat and decay due to lack of ethical behavior.

Yet, underlying this is a large movement of people who believe in the goodness of All and are working towards a Oneness with humanity.

The next natural step in our consciousness evolution according to these prophecies will be the laying down of power — personal, corporate, political. It is the coming together of Eastern and Western philosophies. It is acceptance and tolerance for individuals.

There are those who interpret the predictions of these and other prophecies as an apocalyptic destruction of the planet. But what if these prophesized next wars are already being fought on this planet? What if it is instead, a battle between those who see the world as a frightening, dualistic place of terrorism and terrorists and those who believe in the ultimate good of creation and of mankind and who truly understand, "I am another you."

The survivors of the next great war could be those who surrender the self serving cloak of dualism and are capable of acknowledging our Oneness.

What I do to you I also do to me.

The Law of Attraction cannot work to your advantage within an attitude of dualism. You cannot raise your vibration to higher levels if you are living predominately in low-level vibrations of fear, scarcity, anger, hatred, jealousy, competition, or power.

You cannot get to good focusing on what is wrong or bad. You cannot get to wealth focusing on debt or scarcity. You cannot get to happiness focusing on your sorrow. You cannot get to reason, love, or peace by hating and killing your neighbor. It is impossible.

In the great Cycle of Ethics and Spirituality, you give up the temptation to judge and compete. It is in this new consciousness, you awaken to the interconnectedness of all, and to the true power of the Law of Attraction.

17

Shift in global consciousness?

Examine this list of trends to see if they help you determine if a shift in consciousness is already happening. This list was included in an article by Deepak Chopra for a British magazine called *Resurgence* and reprinted in *ODE Magazine*.

How many of these trends, not present 15, 20, or more years ago are now part of your life? The list comes from Deepak Chopra; the comments are mine.

Manifestation of desires will be talked about as a real phenomenon. Isn't that exactly what we are doing in our study of the Law of Attraction? We talk about being clear about what you want and having the right vibration to allow you to manifest whatever you desire. More and more people are interested in learning these skills.

Alternative forms of healing both physical and psychological will become commonplace. Are there any of you who are not taking vitamins or natural herbs, using magnets or other energy technologies?

Meditation will become mainstream. Not only are more and more people taking up meditation, but the Transcendental Meditation organization is now offering it to schools around the country in a program called Invincible Schools, and educators are listening.

New communities of belief will arise. Consider the people being drawn to materials, books, and seminars on topics of spirituality and personal growth. Look at the people who are writing about spirituality from a scientific point of view. These are quantum physicists, biologists, and even medical doctors.

Wisdom traditions will grow to embrace the great spiritual teachings at the heart of organized religion. We shared some of the ancient Mayan and Hopi spiritual teachings and astrological predictions. There is also a growing interest in the West in many of the Eastern teachings like the Vedas, Islam, and Buddhism. Out of these wisdoms and through our selected retention of the teachings of organized religion will emerge wisdom traditions formulated to meet the spiritual needs of today's individual.

Faith will no longer be seen as an irrational departure from reason and science. See who is writing about faith today! It is the scientists and quantum physicists who are becoming the new spiritual voices of the day. Faith and surrender are fundamental to using the Law of Attraction. Faith and surrender are also the same tenets taught by religious leaders. Throughout this book we have encouraged you to think and act in faith. Trust your instincts and intuition. Faith is a right-brain function and you will be called upon in this future reality to develop greater functionality of creative, intuitive right-brain elements.

Elements of the miraculous and paranormal will be widely acknowledged. Lynne McTaggart's highly successful book, *The Field*, brought together the works of many independent researchers who are looking at how the paranormal is, in fact, normal and can be learned and practiced by anyone who desires. Her latest book, *The Intention Experiment*, expands on those studies. Quantum mechanics computers will enable greater research into the paranormal — providing explanations that will make the paranormal "normal."

Prayer will be seen as real and efficacious. Research has also been done on the power of prayer. Although the studies are inconsistent, as the conditions are difficult to replicate, there is a strong link between what is called "holding an intention" and the power of prayer. The impact of intention is being studied by scientists and believed to be real and efficacious.

People will regain a connection to their souls. Ten years ago I would not have thought I would be setting up a company about Soul and teaching what I am today. I realize I am part of an energy movement that has swept me in this direction as it has for many others.

Individuals will find answers inwardly to their deepest spiritual questions. They will believe in their private answers and live accordingly. Observe the increase in self help books and seminars on spirituality and personal life journeys and the people seeking this information who would never have frequented new age bookstores in the past!

Gurus and other spiritual authorities will wane in influence. Many people who have not belonged to organized spiritual groups are seeking and finding their own way in more flexible arrangements with likeminded people. This is fueled by communication on the Internet and also reflects a world that does not operate through power dominance. It is a roundtable of influence and self discovery, free of judgment and dualism, respecting the rights and beliefs of all people.

18

From power to spirituality

How do we make the transition from a cycle dominated by power to one of ethics and spirituality? The knowledge of how to apply the Law of Attraction may be gaining popularity at this time as we intuitively seek to make the transition from the Cycle of Power to the Cycle of Ethics and Spirituality. Imagine a life without power and control over others. Is a future respecting others for their chosen beliefs, a future of abundance, of joy and peace, something worth pursuing?

Western thinking tends to be more power-centered, logical, and analytical, while Eastern thinking leans toward more spiritual, meditative, intuitive, and holistic tenets. We in the West need to embrace more right-brain thinking to achieve a healthy balance of left and right hemispheres. More right-brain activity connects you to energy fields where genius, creativity, and inspiration reside. It is all about balance. This shift in consciousness from power to spirituality can be accelerated by the following:

Live in Gratitude. Gratitude is the turning point from living an inner-directed self-absorbed life, to becoming a loving, abundant soul. As soon as one pauses to count one's blessings, a shift in consciousness occurs. The need for personal gain at any cost, so often associated with exercising power, is diminished as one puts into the larger context things one already possesses that bring true happiness.

Abandon duality. Since the symbolic casting out from the

Garden of Eden, we have had duality ruling our consciousness. This worldview of scarcity/abundance, right/wrong, good/evil is inconsistent with a transition to a world of ethics and spirituality. We want to evolve our consciousness to a level existing prior to the Fall, a return to a consciousness of bliss. Can any of us truly believe a creator would only allow a few of his creations to be saved? Can a loving spirit believe only a few pious people have got it right and are worthy of salvation? Perhaps these ego-related ideas have crept into our psyche from a desire to exercise power and control: "Only those who believe in my religion will be saved from hell." Its ideal does not seem to be part of a loving, cosmic plan of higher consciousness. I would ask, "Why is it possible for you to accept people are hardwired to be evil, cruel, and power-centered? Can you accept we inherently have a loving nature? Look into the eyes of every newborn and tell me...do you see anything but love, hope, and trust? Is it not more likely we CHOOSE to act through competition, power, violence, and corruption? Can we also CHOOSE to live in peace and harmony and love?"

To make the transition to this way of living in a higher energy consciousness, you give up power over others. You let them experience their own journey and trust you do not have to control everything or fix anything. Ridding ourselves of a dualistic mind is to let go of our judgments. Are you willing to accept others regardless of their race, religion, political persuasion, expecting only that they hold an attitude of love and peace?

Develop your Intuition. Accessing intuition is a highly-developed right-brain capability. Intuition allows for the thought connections of the abundant energy field to enter your mind. In intuitive thought, you find creative and rich solutions to what you have to DO. Yes, you do have to do something. This is not a matter of asking, then sitting around and waiting. In practicing the

Law of Attraction, you become an active participant in the process but the action you take is with ease, grace, trust, and surrender. It comes from that "quiet place." It is your universal energy voice, the language of vibration. Your intuition should more appropriately be referred to, not as your sixth sense, but as your first sense! It is your emotional guidance system. When we learn to live through a highly-advanced intuitive voice, we are listening to the voice of spirit and are wisely guided in our actions.

Can we successfully evolve? It can only happen by a coming together of likeminded people. We do not need consensus. Maharishi Mahesh Yogi maintained that, at most, one percent of a population transcending to highest consciousness can cause a significant shift in socio-economic conditions for the masses. The power of totally enlightened consciousness may be beyond our ability to fully understand or attain. However, we can start by accepting that each of us, holding positive thoughts and striving towards higher consciousness, can bring about personal change and change for humanity — not marching and flag-burning or impeaching, just THINKING about a better future. Do you want a better future for yourself, your children, and the planet? Developing your skills to live in a cycle of ethics and spirituality and applying those skills through the Law of Attraction has the potential to bring to you a whole new world. It not only gives you the new car or the new clients you want. It gives you and humanity, the future we all long for — a future of inner peace and happiness.

19
Duality

The Planetary Cycle of Power has been dominated for the past 400 years by attitudes of duality. Dualism has some of its origins in the biblical story of Adam and Eve with the dichotomies of right/wrong and good/evil, and inclusion/exclusion. When Newton proposed his theories of classical physics that everything was matter and, therefore, separate from everything else, the relationship man had experienced as an interconnected being with his God, with nature and with each other was suddenly dismissed and dualism was firmly entrenched. Science was now the new God.

A sense of being separate from all that IS was further compounded by the Copernican revelation that the earth and humans on it were no longer the center of the universe. Then, by Darwin's theory of relativism stating we were just another species, no longer divinely ordained. And also, by Descartes, who extended this separation to include a mind operating in isolation from the body.

Understanding the dualistic "we/they–right/wrong–good/evil" worldview is important to working within the Law of Attraction. To reach abundance and success and attract good things, you vibrate at higher levels of frequency or consciousness, devoid of dualistic, competitive, scarcity thoughts. You cannot attract love in an attitude of hate. You cannot attract abundance when living in fear of scarcity. You cannot attract joy from an attitude of hopelessness.

This Newtonian, pre-deterministic thinking creates a culture of angst, depression, stress, and hopelessness. Somewhere deep inside, this does not resonate as truth. This consciousness struggle is partly to blame for the widespread feelings today of burnout and alienation.

Release the thoughts and feelings no longer serving you, free yourself from dualistic thinking, and consciously attract a life recapturing youthful hopes and dreams. You have the power to create joy and peace.

In exploring the prophecies we address this concept of duality because it is inherent to the culture of the Great Cycle of Power. "I am more powerful than you;" "I have the right to more abundance than you;" "I must seize my share before it is all gone." Duality is also the belief that what you have been taught — what you know — is the only truth. It means for you to be right, someone else has to be wrong. It is not the attitude inherent to a culture of Ethics and Spirituality.

Ridding ourselves of a damaging dualistic, judging attitude is essential for the Cycle of Ethics and Spirituality, and integral to mastering the Law of Attraction. Freedom from dualism — nonduality — takes you to higher consciousness where you attract greater abundance. Learning to be in non-duality requires listening, learning, and respecting all ideas and differences. From openness you pick and choose the ideas that serve you best while respecting the rights of others to choose different ideas!

> Your Second Insight. Live a life of non-duality seeking the best in, and for, yourself and all around you.

Getting started

Personal change involves becoming informed, then integrating the new ideas and behaviors into your daily routine, and finally, internalizing them, so they are who you BECOME. It is all about you BEING MORE!

Can you release your need to be in control? Can you let go and allow others to have their differences without judging, offering only respect and curiosity?

For one day be open to all comments, ideas, and possibilities. Surrender the need to judge, debate, or evaluate others. Believe each comment was made from love and respect, and return the same in kind.

Observe how often you may have been inclined to force your ideas or values on others. Write down your feelings about this experience in a journal at the end of the day.

Monitor the signs of the struggle of the power cycle fighting to remain in control — in your city, country, or the world. Also note the signs of a greater demand for ethics and spirituality. Writing these observations in a journal gives you an interesting perspective over a period of time.

Summary

Prophecies and duality

Awareness of the divine cosmic plan contained in the ancient prophecies helps us to understand how learning the skills to use the Law of Attraction are necessary to make a transition to higher consciousness.

The Mayan Calendar shows a history of evolution of the planet from the first cell to the highest level of consciousness.

Hopi, Mayan, Biblical, and astrological prophecies all suggest we are at a point of spiritual renaissance.

Understanding ourselves as energy within the natural Law of Attraction is necessary for our participation in this renaissance.

We need to balance left- and right-brain thinking and global hemispheres of power.

Developing our skills of intuition enables us to manifest through the Law of Attraction.

The time has come to rid ourselves of dualistic thinking and the need for power and control, recognizing instead that, "I am another you."

The next great phase of evolution is about ethics and spirituality.

Now it is time for you to apply the Law of Attraction and your understanding of the nature of quantum physics to consciously create your ideal future by learning the BE – HAVE – DO method.

BE. Clear about who/what you intend to be — INTENTION

HAVE. The right vibration to attract what you intend — TRANSCENDING CONSCIOUSNESS

DO. Inspired action — INTUITION

In these next three segments, you are given the techniques to create through the power of your intention, the expression of your gratitude, and the magic of your intuition.

<u>BE</u>
Intention

Intention is a force that exists in the universe. When a sorcerer (those who live in the Source) beckon intent, it comes to them and sets up a path for attainment which means that sorcerer's always accomplish what they set out to do.
    – *Carlos Castaneda*, The Teachings of Don Juan

20

Conscious intention

The first step in our BE – HAVE – DO method is, **BE CLEAR ABOUT YOUR INTENTION**. Focus your thoughts on what you INTEND to attract into your life. Creating a conscious intention is holding fast to a preferred thought until you manifest that which you are thinking about.

Throughout this book as I refer to thoughts, you may be wondering, "Where do beliefs fit into all of this?" A belief is a thought repeated over and over. It becomes an entrenched thought. To keep terminology consistent I refer only to thoughts while appreciating a belief is a repetitive thought.

Thoughts are integral to the Law of Attraction. So, where do our thoughts come from? Can we be conscious creators of our thoughts? Do our thoughts influence others around us? Can we manifest and shape our lives just through the power of our thoughts? Understanding the source of our thoughts and holding a sustained thought can be hard work!

All too often, we subscribe to "second-hand thoughts," placed in our minds by the media, our friends, families, or society. We may not question whether they are serving us well. We may not consider that we can replace them. We have taken these thoughts on, given them a home, accepted them as truth, and these unevaluated thoughts are shaping our lives. Ask yourself, "Is this truth? Or is this something someone else encouraged me to think because it served a purpose for them? Is this what I think because my parents, my teachers or my friends may also have had these same thoughts? Is this really what I choose to think?"

One of my personal coaching clients is a high energy, delightful woman who is readily able to manifest abundance in all areas of her life — except finances. We were puzzled. Why should financial abundance be such a stumbling block for her? One day in a discussion of the things for which she was grateful, we unveiled it! She was recalling her childhood in a large family with limited funds. She realized the word gratitude was most frequently used in the context of, "Who are you to ask for more? You should be GRATEFUL for what you have!!" The thought planted in her youthful, impressionable mind was that she should not aspire to greater abundance than she currently possessed. Once these thoughts, not of her choosing, were revealed, they needed to be replaced. The word "gratitude" also carried a low vibration for her, so it too, needed to be replaced with a higher vibrational word. Shortly after choosing to hold new thoughts about her abundance worthiness, she attained one of her major income goals.

We may lack clarity about what we think, and our life unfolds with the same level of uncertainty. Are you waffling, sometimes thinking you want success, and other times wanting to remain in your current state even though it may not please you? If this is happening for you, try this for forty-eight hours! Write down your thoughts. Ponder them. Do they really represent what you want? If not, replace them with thoughts of your choosing. This may seem a bit tedious but make an effort to do this for as long a period as you can. Be mindful of any thoughts that are dualistic in nature — "If I have to be right, then someone else has to be wrong;" "If I am good, then someone else is bad;" "For my religion to be right, everyone else's has to be wrong." These thoughts can be well hidden in the depths of your psyche. They may make you fearful of being tolerant or open to someone else's religion, politics, ethnicity, or belief systems. Wouldn't you want to be fully aware of the thoughts that may be creating your world?

Creating a conscious intention requires being aware of our thoughts, replacing them, if necessary, with our preferred thoughts, and developing the skills to hold an intention. Holding an intention and being able to manifest is like playing the piano. We can all learn to do it. Some of us will be better at it than others but it can be learned. It requires technique and practice. This technique, more than any other skill, is something you want to devote some time to developing. It has the potential to give you the life of your dreams.

Most of the time, we create unconscious intentions, and become upset and frustrated with what we receive. We may not realize when we worry about something that might happen, we are actually unconsciously INTENDING it! When I worry about not being successful in my job interview, I am unconsciously intending the interview to go badly. Our preoccupation with the parts of our lives that do not please us only assures us of getting more of the same! Are you having financial problems? If you are constantly thinking about the money you do not have, you continue on without attaining the financial wealth you desire. Are your relationships failing? You are likely thinking about all the past failures in your relationships, living them over and over like a bad movie. You will get more of the same.

It may be hard to accept personal responsibility for your current reality but at the same time, it is liberating to know you can change your present circumstance through your thoughts and intentions. When you consciously choose what you want to intend into your life, you change your results, and you become a Conscious Attractor!

21

Be a Conscious Attractor

What does it mean to be a Conscious Attractor? Who are these people? How do they do what they do? They can be anyone, of any age, ethnicity, political persuasion, or religion. But there are some distinguishing attributes. They seem to live a charmed life. They are always living in the Law of Attraction. People describe them as being "so lucky." Good things come their way. They seem happy almost all of the time. I have been delighted to meet many of them. Many more of us are developing our skills to greater and greater degrees because we are enchanted with the lifestyle of these attractors.

Kim is a Conscious Attractor.

She attended my Attracting Success seminar and watched the DVD *The Secret*. Kim said, "I GOT IT!" She immediately started living in the Law of Attraction, telling as many people as she could. She explains, "I did not know for sure how it worked or what I really needed to do, but I was convinced it was real. I used the phrase "Wouldn't it be great if…" and I would fill in the blank. First it was parking spaces, then checks in the mail, then I thought — how about attracting a new building for my business?"

She decided to try what she believed would be the BIG TEST.

This is what I knew I wanted: a building with at least eight parking spaces, easy access on a well-traveled street, peaceful, cheerful place with a good-sized meeting room, overhead door for loading and storage, and I had to pay for it with cash. I had no idea where that was going to come from. My daughter located a building for us on the second try and I asked the realtor what was next. I made an offer of $55,000 cash, which was accepted (the owner wanted $79,900). I had about 30 days until the closing to come up with $50,000 (I put $5,000 on deposit). I only had about $13,000 in the bank. I just kept believing the money would be there and picturing us being in the building and using it. To this day, I am still not sure where all the money came from. I worked. I talked. I was excited and it just showed up. On the morning of the closing I was still short $4,000 — still believing that it would show up. I cleared my mind and let it go. My favorite mind-clearing thought is "Be still and know that I am God." As soon as I cleared my mind, I got an inspired thought and called a customer who was thinking about purchasing some software. I asked if they would like to go ahead and order and give me a check now. They said, "Yes!" It was $4,000!

Conscious Attractors exude confidence. Solutions come to them whenever they need them. They sparkle with laughter and delight as synchronicities happen again and again. For them the glass is always half full. No time is wasted on "what if" or "I wish it would have." When bad things happen, they ask, "What was I to gain from this experience?" Then they are ready to move on with confidence, knowing the things they are waiting to manifest are just around the corner. Does this suggest they are repressing their emotions or that they are in denial? Not at all! They feel the hurt, they feel the pain, but they know they have a choice to let the pain or hurt consume them or they can focus on the good they can take from the experience and hold on to that "beacon of goodwill" as the pain subsides.

You may have heard the story of the little boy who desperately wanted a pony. One day, his father found him digging with a little shovel in a huge pile of manure that had been removed from the barn. When asked what he was doing, the little boy replied, "Well, with this much manure, I just know there has to be a pony in here somewhere."

That is the thinking of Conscious Attractors. They hold a positive attitude that every moment brings them evidence what they want is in the process of becoming. They know their intention will ultimately materialize, and as each life experience unfolds, they are open to the possibilities. They are continuously observing to see if now is "the right moment."

You know it is the right intention and the right moment by the way it feels. Intention holds a special knowing coming from deep within us. It is a feeling of calm and certainty. You can set goals and scrunch up your face and wish with all your might for what you want, but that is not intention. Intention is a special connection deep in your soul, giving you a sense of calm and excitement that what you are wanting will manifest. It requires clarity, but it does not have to be continually pushed against to make it happen.

Conscious Attractors have the ability to flow with their low feelings. They do not resist them. They do not fret over them. They do not find someone else to blame. They recognize the emotion for what it is, acknowledge its source, and shift their vibration by searching for the good in the situation. All the while, they are thankful for the learning this experience is giving them.

Conscious Attractors know when they really desire something, when they really intend it, when they hold an emotion of delight, it manifests. Things that otherwise would never have happened begin to occur. First, they consciously choose what they want to think. Their thoughts are very clear. Conscious Attractors know what they want.

The idea of clearly asking for what you desire and expecting to have it appear is not new and revolutionary — it is promised to you. But you do have to ASK.

Ask and it will be given to you; seek, and you will find; knock, and it will be opened to you. For everyone who asks receives, and he who seeks finds, and to him who knocks, it will be opened.
– Matthew 7:7,8

Your full success in becoming a Conscious Attractor will be realized as you move along the path toward higher consciousness, abandoning attitudes of competition, scarcity, and separateness, living instead with an integrated worldview respecting the rights of all to access joy, abundance, and peace.

22

Mastering intention

A Conscious Attractor has perfected intention.

Intention requires commitment. Be 100% committed to your intention. The steps we recommend in developing your intention include:

> be specific about what you want;
> feel your intention;
> visualize your intention;
> muscle test your intention — we teach you how;
> focus and hold a high vibration; and
> engage all six senses in the manifesting.

But most of all, commit 100%. We are a society reluctant to make commitments. Wedding vows are often rewritten to change the commitment from "as long as we both shall live" to "as long as we both shall love." A bit of an escape clause, just in case I don't quite feel like keeping this commitment one day! Or equally unable to make commitment, are the folks you invite to a meeting or social occasion who say, "I'll see what I can do." Translation: "If nothing better comes up, I will be there!" Are you able to make a decision and commit 100% to keeping it? Do you ask for and expect the same of others?

Here is an interesting exercise often used to reinforce the absolute power of intention. The question is this: "What is the relative importance in this formula of intention to action?"

The formula is: Intention + Action = Results

Assume action IS being taken. But the question is, "How significant to your result is the action you choose versus your intention?" If my intention is to go to work on Monday, does it matter if I choose to walk, skip, ride the bus, or take a train?

Or does it matter more that I am 100% intended to make this happen versus 99% intended to make this happen? We spend a great deal of time concerning ourselves about the best way to do something when we should be focused on, "What is my emotional vibration? What is my level of commitment to the result? How passionate am I about it?"

If we are 100% intended, a way appears. If arriving at my result is what I want, it matters less what action I take. What does matter is that I hold a 100% commitment to make it happen. There is no room to pull back or give up. However, if I am only 99% committed, there is one percent chance I will give up and won't fulfill my intention. If you want to create something in your life, your intention must be 100%!

Without 100% commitment, it is very difficult to achieve success and virtually impossible to attract success. If you have less than 100% commitment, you waffle on your focus. One day you start attracting and the next day you give up. You are plugging and unplugging into your intention and failing to make the sustained connection that attracts results.

What are your intentions? Are you 100% committed?

Intention requires clarity of what you want to have happen or manifest in your life. Your intention is the dream of what you long to manifest. You experience it as a calm, inner knowing. Develop your dream. Gently hold and embrace that dream with every part of your being. Use it as a beacon against any negativity that comes your way. It is a scientific fact — you will achieve! If you have stopped dreaming or rarely built dreams, now is the time to decide what you really want. Now is the time to really envision what you want for your life.

If you knew whatever you wanted or asked for would be delivered to you, would you ask for that with definiteness and purpose?

Intention requires the skills to visualize and feel. The technique of visualization has helped many athletes achieve peak performance, and it is also essential for peak "intention" performance. Recent studies point out, however, it is more than just visualizing. The feeling of the visualization makes all the difference. Some athletes have no problem seeing themselves going through the actions, but their visualization may at times be clouded by thoughts of uncertainty or doubt. What they may not realize is that it is the feelings or emotions of their visualization that are being entrenched. If they hold anything less than positive feelings, the visualization may be doing more harm than good. The FEELING is more important than the VISUALIZING. Intention is stronger when you FEEL the words — and VISUALIZE your intention.

Intention requires the right environment. Since we are interconnected energy with all animate and inanimate things, the seemingly "external" environment, then, has a direct and significant impact on our physical and mental state. Surrounding ourselves with positive people, selecting and creating an appropriate physical space, and engaging in a wholesome lifestyle are essential to fine-tuning skills to manifest your intention.

Meditation is one technique to set up an environment of calm, relaxed energy flow. It is an effective way to train your mind to block out the ego messages, thoughts, and beliefs no longer serving you. In this state, both brain hemispheres are increasingly balanced, a reflection of inner peace and happiness. Matthieu Ricard, son of a French philosopher and co-author with his father of a book titled *The Monk and the Philosopher*, has been pronounced the happiest man in the world. Based on MRI scans of his prefrontal lobes, his balanced brain functions show little sign of negativity. He attributes this to logging more than 10,000 hours in meditation!

You also benefit from having a special place to meditate on a regular basis. This physical space becomes entrained to the vibration or intention you hold, further strengthening the power of your intention.

The level of negative ions in the atmosphere is another factor that influences the power of intention. There is a relationship between levels of either positive or negative ions and brain wave frequencies. Storms, high winds, and low visibility conditions create high positive ions and are not conducive to developing a strong intention. Being around water or a walk in nature, puts you in an environment of high negative ion activity. This high negative ion environment enhances your ability to intend your reality. In her book, *The Intention Experiment*, Lynne McTaggart concludes, "I began to view Intention as a vast energetic relationship involving the sun, the atmosphere and earthly and circadian rhythms." Intention seems to be much more than just holding a thought!

Intention requires having faith. Knowing a little about the science behind the Law of Attraction may be intellectually helpful to developing faith (a left-brain approach), but you must also have faith in a higher organizing power of the universe (a right-brain approach). Do you have total faith what you think about, you can bring into your life? Do you have faith it is not up to you to figure it out and instead, are you ready to hand it over to the inspiration and intuition residing in the universal energy field? Can you truly turn over to your Higher Self? What is your belief of One Source energy, God, Higher Self, or whatever term fits your belief system? Having faith and surrendering to your Higher Self is fundamental to all spiritual philosophy. Faith comes from a deep place of inner or intuitive knowing and accepting. Faith comes from more right-brain thinking. Hold a positive feeling for success, hold a mental picture of you as that successful person, and it will manifest.

Embrace the essence of your intention with passion, knowing the details do not need to be defined and certainly not repeated over and over. Frequent repetition may weaken, not strengthen, your vibration. You may be feeling fearful that what you want will not happen so you say, "I have to keep saying it over and over because I do not believe it can happen." If that is the case, your feelings are actually working against what you want to achieve. Putting aside the temptation to work out the specific details once you have established clarity of the dream, desire or intention, and just holding on to the feeling of what you will experience when your intention is realized requires total faith in the process.

Intention is much more than a wish or a desire. It is 100% conviction what you desire will materialize for you. Intention is a skill, and skills require knowledge and practice. You are gaining the knowledge. Now, commit to the practice and you will master the power of intention. Intention works for our individual desires but it can also be amplified when practiced in a group.

23

Collective intention

Over twenty years ago, long before I had the level of understanding I have today about intention, I had firsthand experience with what seems to be the power of a group holding a common 100% intention.

My friend's son was gravely ill and had been in a coma for several weeks. She arranged a prayer session for him, asking everyone who knew him to pause for a moment at nine on a Monday evening and send their best thoughts for a healthy and complete recovery. Although I knew this was probably a nice thing to do, I really believed it would be more beneficial for my friend than for her teenaged son. The prognosis for his recovery was very bleak. I felt the real value of such an exercise was in her knowing she was supported by friends who would do whatever she asked to show their love and support. The idea this could actually have an impact on the recovery of her son .... Well, I was too analytical for that kind of thinking.

I was traveling for business at the time and knew I would have to keep a mental note to hold her son in my thoughts on that night. I was in a car driven by the senior official of the company. We had finished a day of meetings in one town, had dinner, and were now on our way to another community three hours away, where we would hold similar meetings on the following day. As we drove into the west, the sun was just starting to set, as it does rather late in summer evenings in the northern part of our province. The sky was a beautiful and somewhat unusual color of red and purple. I must admit, with the travel plans and the day of meetings, I had forgotten this was the day I had promised to be part of an intention group for the recovery of my friend's son.

Suddenly, I heard a ringing in my ears. It was like a huge football field full of fans chanting his name and saying, "You can do it! You can do it! You can do it!" And then, the words to a song started going through my mind: "When the deep purple falls, over sleepy garden walls and the stars begin to twinkle in the night. In the midst of a memory, you wander on back to me, breathing my name with a sigh…"

It was over in an instant. My eyes welled up with tears, and I looked straight ahead into the very purple-colored sky. The sun began to dip into the horizon. I glanced over at the watch on my colleague's arm and noted the time; it was 9:03 p.m. The next day, I received an excited call from my friend. Her son had come out of the coma that evening, and the first word he said was "Mom."

"In the midst of a memory, you wander on back to me, breathing my name with a sigh…"

At the time, I thought it was a rather interesting coincidence. It never occurred to me perhaps we were on to something duplicable for anyone and for anything we wanted to manifest. Now research on entanglement and the power of intention suggest this was more than just coincidence. Distance makes little difference to the power of our intention. All the people involved were physically in different locations, and some, like me, were several hundred miles away but our thought energies were "entangled."

Many studies have been conducted on the impact of group intention through meditation or prayer groups. One of the largest experiments ever to be undertaken on group intention is currently being conducted by Lynne McTaggart and Dr. Gary Schwartz. Coordinated through the sale of her book, *The Intention Experiment*, McTaggart and a team of scientists have called upon individuals to meditate or hold a prescribed, focused intention at a specific time. These intentions are a series of web-based experiments that "will demonstrate that your intentions, your thoughts can change something we accept as governed by the laws of nature."

> On Sunday, March 11th, 2007, at 5pm GMT, the 400 people in a conference hall in London, England, started to intend for a leaf to glow and glow. That leaf, by the way, was some 6,000 miles away in a laboratory in Arizona.

> The chosen leaf glowed so brightly that the physicists monitoring it were astonished by how luminous it became. Now those remarkable results are soon to be published in a prestigious science journal.
> http://book.theintentionexperiment.com

You may want to go to this website to participate in future experiments as these intention researchers continue to explore this phenomenon.

There certainly is anecdotal evidence of the power of prayer or the power of group intention. The communion of likeminded people is significant. Although there are many things we can change through individual conscious intention, some things come to us as the collective creation of society, and can only be changed by changing the collective consciousness.

Collective intention may also provide a possible response to the detractors of the concept of the Law of Attraction who say, "Surely you cannot say this person deliberately attracted this awful experience?" It is important to remember our quantum energy interconnectedness in responding to this question. Western thought still dwells on our separateness and individual nature. In quantum reality we are not isolated entities. What happens to one is a result of what is happening to the whole. Things may happen to individuals through the collective focus of society. They are victims of our collective consciousness. We should learn from these ill-fated events and adjust our collective thinking accordingly. For example, a society fixated on fear of terrorism experiences more terrorism, and there are innocent victims. A society bombarded with images of rape and murder manifests these crimes and takes innocent victims.

We live in a power-based world collectively perpetuating a belief there are limited amounts of everything. We have unconsciously accepted as truth there should be "haves" and "have-nots," "winners" and "losers" in the world. As long as we are influenced by scarcity thinking, we live in scarcity. That is unconscious intention. When we see violence in our neighborhoods, we build more barricades and security gates entrenching our fear and ensuring we attract more neighborhood violence. When we experience violent crimes in our schools we talk about metal detectors and security guards, perpetuating a climate of fear and attracting more fearful events.

Wouldn't it be worth testing this concept of collective intention by coming together with like-minded people who hold a vision of a different way of being to see if through our thoughts and expectations we can create instead a benevolent society? The Observer creates whatever the observer expects!

24

Holding intention for someone else

*Treat people as if they were what they ought to be and you help them
become what they are capable of being.*
– Johann Wolfgang von Goethe, German philosospher

If a group of people can have an impact on an outcome through
their concentrated thoughts, is it possible for an individual to
hold an intention for another person? Is it possible someone
else's good intention for you may be as powerful as you holding
them yourself!

One man in Sydney, Australia, chose to do just that and established the Choir of Hard Knocks. He invited all street people who
relied on crime to support their drug habits to join his choir. The
choir has performed to sellout audiences at the Sydney Opera
house. He changed his thoughts about street people by choosing
to see possibility and promise, and they became what he believed
they could be.

If we accept the quantum realities of our energy connection to
one Source and we accept the Observer creates reality, we should
be able to assume you can hold an intention for someone else. By
holding an expectation of the event or relationship, you are influencing how an event or relationship may unfold.

Some of the clients I coach are dealing with strained relationships with teenagers who are testing their boundaries and independence. The result is often a power clash. The parents are constantly anticipating the next blow up. They expect the teen will not keep a curfew or obey the family rules. We know the Observer gets what they expect! My answer to their questions about what they can do to get responsible behavior at times astounds them.

My advice has nothing to do with the teenager and everything to do with the parents. The parents are encouraged to change their thoughts and hold a new intention for the teen. Instead of thinking about all the things that could go wrong, I ask them to think instead about their teen in the highest possible light. Whenever a worrisome or negative thought emerges, replace it with a higher order thought, such as "My son (daughter) makes great decisions, s/he is loving and kind and acts in a responsible way." It is amazing how quickly the children "change!" By altering the energy matrix between parent and child, new attitudes or behaviors are able to crystallize in response to the higher vision being held.

If holding a positive thought or vision for someone can actually result in a change in how that person becomes in our relationship, can we also hold thoughts for them to help them manifest their desires when they may not yet hold a strong enough belief in themselves? Can we pool our intentions to help our loved ones?

Our son graduated from medical school in Kingston, Ontario, and wanted to move from his one-bedroom, high-rise apartment he not-so-fondly referred to as a "human filing cabinet," to a more unique accommodation in one of the many beautiful historic buildings in Kingston. He was scheduled to do a surgical residency for another five years and wanted something more suited to his preferred lifestyle and environment. We were there to attend his graduation, so we accompanied him on his search. His intention gained clarity as we viewed properties: two bedrooms or bedroom with den, hardwood floors, well-maintained building, quiet, close to the hospital, parking space and within his budget for the monthly rent.

After several days of searching, he gave up and concluded he would not find anything in his price range to meet his criteria. I, on the other hand, love a challenge, especially when it comes to manifesting intention. On a weekend when he traveled to Toronto, my husband and I set out to attract the perfect place. We decided to drive up and down every street within reasonable distance from the hospital, excluding the two streets he mentioned he preferred but on which he thought the rents would be more than he could afford. After three hours, we were almost tempted to come to the same conclusion he had...but how could I possibly deliver another Soul Abundant seminar if I gave up!

Instead, we decided to take a deep breath, rid ourselves of any limiting thoughts, and allow for inspired thought to happen. I suggested we drive down the streets he expected would be too expensive. Midway down the first street was a beautiful, old, well-maintained building with a tiny cardboard sign in the window on the main floor. I used my cell phone to make the call. Amazingly, the notice had been put up only 30 minutes prior to our calling! Had we started our search here we would have missed it and most likely would not have returned to check again. We viewed the apartment and found it met all criteria. And the rent? Significantly less than he had budgeted!

At times our own light goes out and is rekindled by a spark from another person. Each of us has cause to think with deep gratitude of those who have lighted the flame within us.
  – Albert Schweitzer

We CAN have an impact on others through connected thought. Together we can assist each other to fulfill our dreams. You can actually improve another person's life through the power of your intention!

25

Creating
an intention statement

Let's get you started on creating an intention statement for an area of your life where you want to see different results. You may be tempted to skip this step in the process thinking, "I know what I want. I think about it all the time." If you are thinking about it all the time, it may be that you are actually thinking about it in the context of its scarcity. "I want to get more income." This thought can really be a focus on the income you do not have. If you stress against it and constantly keep running this thought through your mind, you are reminding yourself of what you do not yet have. The feeling with this thought will be one of scarcity and result in attracting more scarcity. This is the subtlety of the Law of Attraction that escapes most new learners. It is the vibration of the feeling that attracts.

Intention is a skill to be learned. You are the pianist and these are the dreaded but necessary scales. Take time to learn them. And the rest will come easily for you! I can assure you if you go through each and every step you will avoid the disappointments faced by those who think that just being aware is enough. You will avoid unexpected outcomes like one of my participants experienced at a course I delivered in Ottawa, Canada.

At the end of the course, a gentleman came up to me with a collage he had created several years earlier. On the collage was a magazine clipping of well-built man with six-pack abs, clad only in a tiny swimsuit, his body painted gold from head to toe. The gentleman put the clipping on his collage to represent the fitness and better body tone he wanted to achieve. In his other hand was a photograph. He extended it to me. It was a photograph of him. He was standing on a wooden box dressed only in an adult-size diaper with a bow and arrow in his hand and his tummy still less firm than the clipping on his collage! He had been cast as Cupid in a play produced by his drama group. His entire body was painted in gold paint from head to toe! It seems his focus had been less on the six-pack abs he wanted — and more on the golden body! Learn to be clear what it is you are asking for!

Developing My Intention Statement (Appendix B):

What I do not want. Select an area of your life where you want to change your results: a career, relationship, home, lifestyle, health, or finances. Once you have selected the area you want to work on, start by listing what is currently in that part of your life that you DO NOT WANT. By listing all the things that you do not want, you rule them out and assure they won't creep into the final picture and surprise you! With your DO NOT WANT list as your guide, you can create a list clearly reflecting your preferences by shifting now to...

What I do want. Move from what you DO NOT WANT to what you DO WANT, by taking each item and carefully looking for its polar opposite. If I DO NOT WANT pain, then, what I DO WANT is "a strong, healthy body." When you have finished transferring the negatives to the positives, come up with a ritual to destroy the negative list.

Several years ago I shared a ritual for letting go of what you don't want and welcoming what you do want with some friends. They faithfully practiced this New Year's Eve ritual by burning the "Don't wants" and burying the "Do wants" in a special location. Their lives soon changed from serious financial stress to owning the acreage home of their dreams.

Write your intention statement. Now, turn these key word lists into intention sentences each describing with clarity and a high emotional vibration, just what it is you are ordering from the universe. Each key word or phrase on the DO WANT list is made into a sentence written to raise your vibration. Use words that evoke a strong feeling:

"I am elated with my strong, healthy, well-toned body."

Describe your feelings as though what you intend has already happened.

Feel the words. Intention is linked to feelings, so your sentences must contain feeling words that resonate for you. After you have completed writing an intention sentence for each of the key words on your DO WANT list, read each sentence over carefully, reading slowly and aloud. You have likely written the sentences in a left-brain mode because that is how most of us have been taught to write. Your goal is to make them right-brain or emotional statements. Language is very powerful and evokes a vibration. Read each word slowly, savoring the vibration it creates. If you feel a lowering of your vibration, pause and ask, "Which word is lowering my vibration?" You may have written, "I am elated with my pain-free body." It seems that should be what you want, isn't it? And yet, you may find this is lowering, not raising, your vibration.

Each word has its own energy and the word "pain" carries a low vibration no matter who you are. Whether you say "pain-free" or "pain," your body still responds to the negative vibration of the word "pain." Try this again with the word "debt" just to get sense of what I am talking about. This sentence holds a higher vibration when it is changed to read, "I am elated now that my body is healthy and vibrant." or "I am so delighted I have more than enough money for the things and experiences I dream of having." This part of the exercise is very personal. Only you can determine whether the words you have used are right for you and to do that you must rely on getting in touch with your feelings.

Visualize the words. Your sentences are now emotionally vivid. But your right brain and your unconscious work in images. Attracting through conscious use of the Law of Attraction is an activity requiring the awakening of your right-brain capabilities. You want to make certain your intention statement creates a mental picture that delights you. Saying, "I am happy now that I earn $100,000 per year," may create a mental picture. But compare that to, "I am happy now that my art gallery, situated on a cliff with an amazing view of the water and mountains, is bringing me into contact with delightful people and earning $100,000 in profits each year." Or perhaps you don't know yet how you want to earn this money. Perhaps you do not as yet have a dream of the service you will render, but you dream of earning that amount of money. You may be asking, "Can I not set a goal just to attract the money?"

My experience is that the clearer the intention the greater the chance of manifesting quickly. If you do not know what you want to do to earn that money, you might get more of a mental picture by saying something like, "I am so happy now that I am using my talents and skills working with people (or machines, etc.) to have a positive impact on their lives, and my service to them earns $100,000 a year."

Review the sentences you have written. Does each sentence help to create a mental picture? If not, change the language or change the idea. Use creative language. You might also reinforce this step of BEING clear on your intention by cutting pictures or using photos and having fun creating a collage of what it is you are intending to bring into your life. Take every opportunity to dream. In our society, where life tends to be lived on the "surface," we rarely go "inside" to dream a vision or life purpose.

The Law of Attraction is heavily reliant upon imagination. Because we have stopped dreaming or are afraid to dream in case we fail, we are inclined to wait until we are sure we know how to reach our goals. Our goals become mundane extensions of what has been in our past. These are not the exciting, "give me goose bump" dreams. You need the dream. It all begins with the dream. Create a dream that "kicks you out of bed in the morning." Create a dream that propels you through any adversity you may face. Create your preferred life in your mind, and a way to that life will appear. Create dreams regardless of your age! Just Imagine!

If you don't dream, you won't know what to ask for! Go and "kick some tires!" Walk through some show homes. Interview some people who are doing interesting things and who are living exciting lives. Ask them what they love about what they do. Gather information and from that information begin to formulate your life dreams, create a vision of your perfect life, and turn that vision into a 100% intention.

Assess your statement using applied kinesiology. This step is mentioned here so you will remember to include it as part of our intention statement process. Once you have read the applied kinesiology section (Appendix A), you can return to your intention statement and use this muscle-testing technique to determine whether your intention statements are clearly stating what you desire and whether your inner or intuitive self believes the statement to be your truth.

Complete your intention statement. Your intention statement begins with the phrase "I am 100% committed to attracting all I need to BE, HAVE, and DO to fulfill my intention for (subject of your intention)..."

Then, in bullet format, list each of the sentences you have written and tested, and end your intention statement with, "I am filled with Gratitude and I am ready to receive (subject of your intention) — right now." (Appendix B.)

Dating your intention statement. In traditional goal setting you typically set a date for completion or milestones of when you want to achieve results. I am often asked whether one needs to put dates on their intention statement, as in this example:

"It is on or before December 31st, and I am elated with my body that is now at my ideal weight."

The answer to the question of setting dates, as in all the questions you may have with the Law of Attraction, can be answered by asking yourself, "How does that make me feel?" If it gives you a high vibration to set a date, then do so. If the thought of setting a deadline lowers your vibration — then don't! When you tap into intuition you know what is right for you. Another challenge faced with deciding on whether or not to set a date, is the tendency to choose a timeframe based what you know from past performances that you can accomplish in a certain period of time. This scarcity or "past performance" thinking is not the connection to the abundance of the quantum field where huge leaps can happen in a short time.

I prefer to say, "I am Grateful and ready to receive right now!" If for some reason, the things I desire are just around the corner, why make them wait! Test your vibration by assessing, "How does it make me feel when I put a date on my intention?" Or you may use the muscle testing or dowsing techniques from Appendix A to verify an answer. Then choose whichever approach works best for you. You are learning to trust your intuition!

When you have completed your intention statement you now have a clear request for what you want to attract. This process can be repeated for anything you want — a job, business, lifestyle, soul mate, car, life purpose, etc. Developing your intention statement requires time and focus in the beginning, but it shortens the time necessary to manifest what you desire in the long term.

With a clear idea of what you want, your responsibility now is to spend your time holding a feeling or vibration in harmony with your Intention. In the next segment, "HAVE – Transcending Consciousness," are seven factors that contribute to raising your vibration or consciousness to a level where you can attract desirable experiences.

Getting started

Personal change involves becoming informed, then integrating the new ideas and behaviors into your daily routine, and finally internalizing them, so they are who you BECOME. It is all about you BEING MORE!

Use the intention statement process to BE clear about what you want. Go through the steps of DO NOT WANT/DO WANT. Write emotionally charged sentences. Test the "feeling" or vibration of the words. Visualize the words. After reviewing the section on applied kinesiology you can muscle test your intention. Once you are certain you have defined your intentions as clearly as possible, put the paper aside and hold on to your mental vision of success with passion and 100% commitment.

Hold a mental picture and a consistent vibration with that which you want to manifest in your life as you go through your day. Experience it as though it is already happening. Smile and enjoy your "new" life! Hold the vision of what you want as though it has already appeared. Savor that feeling and trust that what you want is now taking form. If you experience feelings of doubt or fear, gently put them aside and remind yourself you are in the process of making it happen. The more you feel as though it has already happened, the faster it will arrive.

Do some research on meditation. If you are not already doing a form of daily meditation, select a method and start your program. Try a variety of methods over time and choose the one that feels right for you. Quieting your mind and being ready to receive is essential to this process.

Create a special space to meditate. The energy of your intention during meditation has an impact on the energy in that space. Appeal to all six senses in setting up that space: sight, sound, smell, taste, touch — and the voice of your intuition.

Seek out other like-minded people who want to study this book. Share each others dreams in an attitude of non-duality — without judgment or evaluation.

Summary
<u>BE</u>
Intention

Intention begins by BEING clear about what you want to manifest.

We were all intended to have the opportunity to explore our full potential.

Conscious Attractors are very clear about what they want to ask for and they know it will manifest for them.

Your energy is entangled with all energies around you.

Let go of the need to control. See yourself as part of a connected whole.

Intention can counter negative external influences.

Create an environment conducive to intention and manifesting.

Align with likeminded people. Become a collectivity, a community for higher consciousness.

Strengthen the intention of a friend or loved one by holding a strong passionate intention for their dream.

Intention MUST BE 100% commitment to manifest.

<u>HAVE</u>
Transcending consciousness

The greatest discovery of my generation is that a human being can alter his life by altering his attitudes of mind.
— William James, philosopher

26

Choose your feelings

At a "dark night of the soul" in my life, I awoke to the full realization of our gift of choice, our free will. I was mentoring some associates who were working very hard, yet success was elusive. I felt responsible and hopeless. The more mired I became in a state of hopelessness, the more my performance began to falter. We were doing the same things that had worked in the past but the activities no longer brought success. I was in a downward spiral. The deeper we slipped collectively into a negative space, the more our performance worsened.

My awakening was to the realization success had little to do with actions. It had a lot to do with feelings. The more hopeless we felt, the more negative the results. One day I realized I could choose to continue to feel hurt and sorry for myself, or I could look for the possibilities these experiences were providing. I could choose different feelings. As soon as I shifted my thoughts and feelings, my whole world started to transform. Through choice, I refused to focus on what was wrong. Nor was I going to allow any more negativity into my life. I started to express gratitude for what I had. I focused on a vision of success as though I was already living that reality. Soon, a world, seemingly dark and bleak, now held hope and promise. Wonderful opportunities aligned with my vibrant new feelings began to present themselves.

Feelings — are you in touch with yours? Learn to acknowledge and label them. As you are examining any decision or action, always ask, "How is this making me feel?" In my coaching with the Law of Attraction I am aware that far too many of us have lost touch with our feelings. We suppress them. We say, "It doesn't matter how I feel; I just need to get this done." We are HUMAN DOINGS, not HUMAN BEINGS!

Before starting any action, tune in to your feelings. Explore them. Start to give them names. Locate where you feel it in your body. "Is this coming from a gut level? Is this from my head? Do I feel it in my heart?" Ask also, "What is there here to celebrate? Is something making me feel badly? Am I listening to or am I suppressing my feelings?" In our society, we communicate a lot about things, and only infrequently about feelings. Coming to terms with our innermost feelings is essential to awakening our BEING and is central to mastering the Law of Attraction.

We can choose our feelings. Our feelings attract our reality. Each of us can become the "dream maker" in our own lives. You can choose to create exuberant joy, playfulness, and laughter! First transform your life through higher levels of vibration and consciousness, and then with gratitude, project that change out into the world to create abundance for others. Begin by transcending to higher levels of consciousness through your choice of feelings...and that will become your life experience.

27

What is transcending?

Transcending: to be greater than, in intensity, and power, to pass beyond the limits of; to surpass — to exist above and be independent of material experiences or the universe.

And what is consciousness? According to neuroscientists, truly understanding consciousness is still one of the greatest unsolved mysteries of our times. Although the brain mechanisms for this complex feedback state are not fully understood, we do know from our experiential data that certain levels of awareness, consciousness and feelings can create a feedback loop that is either constructive or destructive. Higher levels of consciousness hold greater personal and collective power. The idea of thoughts or feelings or consciousness having power, and empty space having energy is relatively new to most of us and sometimes hard to grasp. We live in a sea of powerful energy, and we are part of that power. Our greatest potential to finding solutions to the success and fulfillment we seek will be found not in our "physical might" but in accessing the power of our higher consciousness.

You don't have to attend protest marches or travel to far-off famine-stricken countries to make a difference, although that may be a worthy endeavor. There is so much impact you can have through your personal consciousness once you learn to be attentive to where you are currently vibrating and acquire the skills to raise your vibration. Of course, an obvious question then is, "To raise or transcend — from what — to what?"

That is where The Body Conscious guide on page 123 can be most instructive. Through this guide we define a pathway of consciousness showing the intensity of feelings, ranging from some of the most negative or regressive to the most positive, progressive, or spiritually aligned. This guide can be used to assess where you are and where you want to be. It shows a continuum moving from the darkness of hopelessness, to the light of enlightenment.

Although you may see similarities on The Body Conscious guide to the locations of the chakras of the body, our intention is not to redefine or align with chakras, but to reflect on where in the body one typically experiences certain emotions. Low level vibrations are most often experienced in the lower part of the body. Love projects in the region of the heart. Joy and wonder are most often vocalized, by exercising our voice in the world, or with exclamations of wonder, or songs of joy, so we have shown these emotions at the throat. The highest levels of vibration, inner peace, bliss and enlightenment are shown at the prefrontal lobe, the part of the brain where brain development is associated with the ability to grasp concepts of ethics, morality, and spiritual awakening.

Any upward movement on this scale of consciousness represents a huge jump in personal and global awakening. You experience many of these emotions from time to time but we are looking for the level on the continuum where you expend most of your emotional energy. By pinpointing your dominant vibration on this continuum you can see the higher levels of emotion you can aspire to for spiritual growth.

The Body Conscious guide directs us to where we may need to shift our feelings to start attracting the outcomes we desire. It has also been designed to assist you in identifying and naming the feelings you are experiencing. Consider where in your body you are experiencing an emotional impact. Is it in the head area? — heart? — or gut region? Often we get a bodily sense of our feelings but we don't have a label for them. Refer to the guide and label the emotion you are experiencing. There are many emotions that could have been included on this continuum. The Body Conscious guide lists some to serve as a prompt, localizing and identifying your feelings, and providing a road map moving ever closer to the point of true happiness and fulfillment.

The very lowest vibrational energies can be totally immobilizing. Levels of extreme sadness or hopelessness result in severe clinical depression if protracted for a period of time as all hope is abandoned. The continuum portrays a movement from almost zero life energy to ultimate life energy. As you progress up the continuum, you gain vital energy.

You may question why anger has been positioned on the continuum next to gratitude. These emotions are very different and it may seem like a huge jump! The Body Conscious continuum speculates on the degree of energy emitted by each of the emotional states. Anger possesses high energy, sufficient to move one to take extraordinary levels of action. Unfortunately, these are not usually actions that serve one well, but the emotion is highly mobilizing. Someone in a consciousness of anger has adequate life force energy to also choose to make positive choices. The energy in anger is exponentially greater than that possessed by someone in hopelessness, a state of depletion where the potential to exercise choice is about to be totally abandoned.

If you lose hope, somehow you lose the vitality that keeps life moving,
you lose that courage to be, that quality that helps you go on in spite of
it all. And so, today, I still have a dream.
   – William Wordsworth

HOPELESSNESS! The point at which almost all power is given up, and one succumbs to the most vulnerable, weakened state! Have you ever, even briefly, experienced hopelessness? You can probably now see how, by dropping to this level of emotion, and consequently, by relinquishing all personal power, a point of almost zero life energy is reached – and unfortunately, through attraction, hopelessness attracts more of the same, and remains the reality! Hopelessness is what we will attract more of in this state even though we may not be aware of what is bringing us all these negative experiences. A life crisis occurs when you do not realize what vibration you are transmitting, and you keep getting results that make you unhappy without knowing what or how to change.

This insight came as a revelation to me as I began to see an interconnectedness of seemingly isolated unfortunate circumstances being experienced by some people I was coaching. I discovered in one person grief as a dominant consciousness stemming from several early childhood experiences. Although the individual is loving, generous, and exuberant about life, it is as though she forces these high-vibrational emotions to counterbalance her dominant locked emotion of grief. Her actions are external behaviors inconsistent with the underlying grief consciousness. Consequently grief, the prevailing emotion of her unconscious state, continues to raise its head and send cruel and unexpected grief experiences.

Tune into and identify the feelings you are vibrating. Then do all you can to change your vibration to increasingly higher levels in alignment with the life you choose to live. You change the vibration and a new reality manifests.

The person who sets a goal to make a million dollars a year but is stuck in low level vibrations of anger, fear, and doubt, attracts experiences to give more anger, fear, and doubt, regardless of the stated goal. The alignment to the vibrations of anger, fear, and doubt is guaranteed. He or she may get close to the stated goal with hard work and effort, but something will likely happen to alter the course of events. For example, things are progressing well, and a major contract collapses — anger is rewarded. Or suddenly, strong competition appears — fear is rewarded. Or there is anxiety about the ability to manage an ever-expanding business — doubt is rewarded. The goal of making one million dollars a year seems to be constantly slipping away.

In all three circumstances, the stated goal has been self-sabotaged. The goal-setter is attracting through anger, fear, and doubt. Unless the vibrations are changed, regardless of the stated goal, these prevailing vibrations assure the individual's current state is maintained.

If you are little skeptical about this, do some research on lottery winners. A disproportionate number of them are back to being broke in no time. Is it because they did not know how to handle that much money? Perhaps, but it likely had much more to do with their vibrational level of being in scarcity, of being broke. The universal energy field is still connected to that "broke" vibration and creating more life experiences to keep them in the vibration of scarcity.

To transcend, one needs to be aware of feeling and consciousness levels — acutely aware of those that serve, and those that do not serve, success, fulfillment and true happiness.

Regressive, dualistic emotions. All negative or low levels of consciousness are regressive for the individual and society. They include hopelessness, sadness, shame, guilt, fear, doubt, and anger. These levels range from a total loss of power and control (hopelessness) to obsessive use of power and control (anger). All are emotional manifestations of an attitude of DUALITY. They are a result of our feeling separate from others, of being left out of the abundance we see around us, and disconnected from the love or success we crave. These emotions are counterproductive to spiritual growth. If someone is predominately at a vibration of shame, a higher level of vibration for them might be fear. Fear is a higher level of consciousness on the Body Conscious guide but will fear help you create your vision or bring you joy and abundance? Much greater movement is required to connect with the more fulfilling experiences coming from levels of gratitude and above.

Progressive, non-dualistic emotions. The emotional levels at GRATITUDE and beyond are progressive and constructive to the individual. These are emotions of NON-DUALITY and include acceptance, empathy, love, joy, wonder, inner peace, bliss and enlightenment. These emotions are in alignment with the prophesized Mayan Eighth Great Cycle of Ethics and Spirituality and are capable of attracting fulfilling life experiences.

GRATITUDE and NON-DUALITY are the tipping point and the beginning of seven factors to examine in transcending to ever higher consciousness.

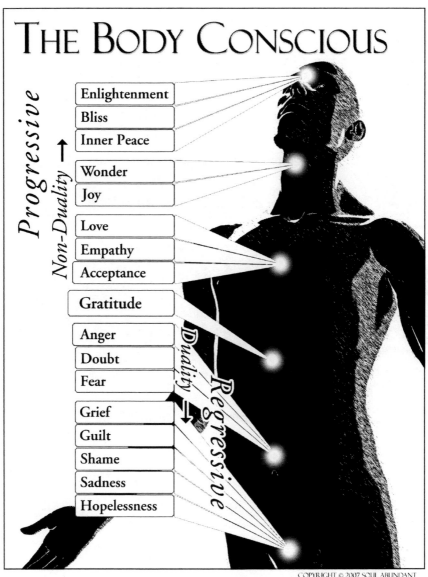

THE BODY CONSCIOUS

Progressive

Non-Duality

Enlightenment

Bliss

Inner Peace

Wonder

Joy

Love

Empathy

Acceptance

Gratitude

Anger

Doubt

Fear

Grief

Guilt

Shame

Sadness

Hopelessness

Duality

Regressive

COPYRIGHT © 2007 SOUL ABUNDANT

Seven Factors Contributing to Higher Consciousness

Factor One: Gratitude

Factor Two: Non-duality

Factor Three: Inspiration

Factor Four: Surrender

Factor Five: New Energy

Factor Six: Good Vibes

Factor Seven: Celebration

28

Gratitude

Factor One

The consciousness tipping point from regressive to progressive vibrations is gratitude — gratitude for the things that are working in your life, however small they may seem at the time. Gratitude for the things that are not working for they serve to awaken you! Gratitude for the life you have been given. Gratitude for the breath you take. Gratitude for the free will you have been given to choose your circumstance.

GRATITUDE. It signals a huge shift from obsessing about what is wrong in your life, to seeing anything and everything that may be working well. Gratitude requires the skill to see the glass as half-full rather than half-empty. It requires you to focus on what you already have that you want more of, and set aside your preoccupations with what you do not have. Moving into gratitude necessitates trusting and surrendering to a higher order of the universe and believing in your connection to that power.

Can you step up and believe in the power within you and within your thoughts? You are more powerful than you have ever believed or imagined. Once you make this decision, you no longer blame your mother, your teachers, your siblings, your boss, your country. It is just YOU. When you make this conscious effort to shift your focus, you are not only deciding to change; you are also deciding to take responsibility for the change!

Imagine starting every staff meeting with a round table of what you have to be grateful for rather than lamenting about the problems for the day. If you begin all meetings with gratitude, you find more energy to dedicate to the solutions. Here is what one IT company experienced when they put this suggestion to work.

> I used your suggestion and started my business meeting by having everyone write down what they are grateful for. Business had been a bit slow and we were looking for work (which is not normal for our business). Instead of talking about that, we talked about what we were grateful for. Within one hour after having this meeting that started with gratitude; we got a call to quote three computers, another for a new server, and two computer repairs! Now that is what I call instant results. I am grateful for your teachings!

Being able to change your reality begins with the realization you are ready to express gratitude, even for the adversity you may be facing. You face your truth. You express gratitude for the aspects of your life that are not going the way they should, perhaps a relationship, overall life frustrations, stress, a career, out of control finances, out of control weight or lifestyle issues. Step out in gratitude and truth, make a decision to take the responsibility to change your life, learn from the experience and begin transmitting a new vibration into the world.

We are here to play a role in evolution by changing our energy to higher and higher levels, for our personal benefit, the benefit of our families and communities, and for future generations. Facing your personal truth and taking responsibility to make a change to live at a higher consciousness makes you an active participant in this game of life.

Sit quietly right now and examine your life as though you are a stranger looking at the person that is your physical being. Look as though you were viewing a movie of your life. Do you have the courage to see what it looks like from that perspective? What is there to be grateful for? There will be much you see that will give you a warm and happy vibration. Focus on that.

Feel the greatness. Be grateful! Just relax and be with that feeling of wonder for who you are. Your very existence is nothing short of a miracle. Experience the joy of the moments for which you are most happy.

And now, gently observe the areas of your life where you want to bring about a change to make these aspects as fulfilling and rewarding as the ones you have just celebrated. Just see them. Observe them for what they are. Do not judge them or yourself. These are just the aspects of your life that are not quite finished. They are areas needing enhancement and evolution. When you do this you cross over a bridge from a dualistic mindset, to the other side to non-duality, openness, non-judgment. You set your feet on the path to greater consciousness and more abundant life experiences. You are becoming gratefully abundant.

> Your Third Insight. Seeking gratitude in all things opens the doors to higher consciousness and true life happiness.

29

Non-duality

Factor Two

A second way to raise or transcend consciousness is releasing dualistic, regressive thoughts and feelings by embracing only the non-dualistic, progressive feelings on the Body Conscious guide starting at Gratitude. Dualistic thinking arises from our sense of separateness. Non-duality on the other hand, is the mode of thinking of the higher levels of consciousness coming from our awareness of our energy connectedness or our Oneness.

Duality has some of its origins in the classical Newtonian theories of the separateness of all things. This way of thinking has dominated education, workplaces, political systems, and is central to a culture based in power. It has influenced the Western world for the past 400 years creating an US against THEM society: "We are the good guys. They are the bad guys. I need to grab my share because there is a finite amount available." Dualistic thinking is a black or white — EITHER/OR — worldview.

Ego is an accomplice in perpetuating duality. What is ego? Ego is the voice of your persona, distinct from your inner voice, the voice of intuition, the voice of your Soul or Spirit. Ego is linked to your physical being and is constantly fighting for its survival. The voice of ego has been shaped by the dualistic idea of separateness: "I am alone. I am in competition. I am not good enough. I am separate from all that is."

In this state of separateness, the ego fights to keep alive. Everything is threatening: "I cannot trust others. I cannot trust nature. I cannot trust God."

Your ego relies on evaluating. It is comparing you to others. It is judging you on who you are or what you have. It is constantly reminding you of your aloneness and prompting a fight or flight response to protect your very being. The most potent fuel keeping ego going is fear and doubt. This little muddle — dualism, ego, fear, and doubt — has kept us entrenched in behaviors so self-absorbed they are destroying the planet and the people on it.

Non-duality on the other hand, resides in the higher consciousness levels. It is a BOTH/AND worldview. There is room for all opinions and options. It is infinite abundance and possibility. "Together we are better." In this non-dualistic interconnectedness, "I am another you;" "The more you help others get what they want, the more you get what you want."

All the higher levels of consciousness — acceptance, empathy, love, joy, wonder, inner peace, bliss, and enlightenment — are possible after one makes the shift to non-duality. You have given up prevailing attitudes of competition and scarcity and the need to have power over others, to control, to be right, to judge, and to compare. You are able to experience things as they are. Be in the moment. Choose original thought. Respect the rights of others to choose their original thoughts.

When you are in non-duality, you find your stress disappears. You do not seek to judge or place blame. You look instead for "What is the opportunity this provides for me and for humankind?" Consider the amazing work of Mother Teresa or any other truly enlightened person. They lived a life of non-duality working without judgment in some of the most destitute situations because they believed goodness and hope lived there also.

Here are some suggestions for quieting the ego voice and dualistic thoughts, so you can make the shift to non-duality.

Write down your self talk. You begin by listening carefully for ego or self-talk messages. What part of your self talk is essentially your ego voice? Once you become aware of what it is, you can begin to isolate those little recordings and replace them. Take the time to write these down over the course of a couple of days. Identify the feelings you associate with each of the thoughts. Are these the thoughts you choose to play over and over in your mind? Are these dualistic thoughts of judging, comparing and evaluating others?

Create new self-talk. Do you talk to yourself in the same manner you would talk to someone you loved very much? Sadly, all too many of us are much harder on ourselves than we would ever be on another person. We are harshly self-critical. Look at the self-talk messages you wrote down in the first part of this exercise. Rewrite any you see that are less than supportive, loving, and kind. Note any that are obviously dualistic in nature. Add at least six new encouraging, loving messages!

Develop a channel changer. Once the thoughts that no longer serve you are isolated and identified, developing a channel changer can be very effective. Create a sentence or series of words you would prefer to hear and use this sentence or phrase every time the ego voice starts to chatter. A channel changer needs to be brief and easy to access. A few key words will do. You create a neural block for those useless messages and set down new pathways with preferable messages. Each time the doubt or fear messages creep into your mind block them quickly with these key words. You will be delighted with how soon you are hearing only your preferred messages.

If your negative self talk is "I am so broke. I never have any money. I worry about paying my bills every month" you want to create a channel changer like "Money is abundantly flowing into my life." Or, an abbreviated version like "money, freely, abundantly," also works. It may seem uncomfortable because your ego voice will argue, "It is not true," but keep a strong vibration as if this has already happened and the universe will align with that vibration. It soon becomes your truth.

Test your channel changer. To make certain you have chosen right-brain, emotionally positive language for your channel changer, use applied kinesiology to verify it is the right energy vibration for you (see Appendix A). Make any adjustments necessary to the wording until you get a strong test. Then start replacing those old useless thoughts with new, inspiring thoughts.

Living in non-duality creates a wonderful sense of calm and moves you closer to inner peace.

30

Inspiration

Factor Three

A third factor for transcending to higher consciousness lies in understanding inspiration and how it differs from motivation.

I am often asked by my personal coaching clients, "How do I motivate my spouse — children — employees — to change the behaviors I do not like?" When I ask if anyone has ever tried to motivate them, they roll their eyes heavenward indicating it was less than a positive experience. Then I ask if anyone has ever inspired them. Their faces light up and stories about great people in their lives instantly come forward. What is the difference between their motivational and inspirational experiences?

I find it is relatively easy for them to discern that when someone tried to motivate them it was driven by the desires of the motivator — for the motivator's reasons — not theirs. You may want to motivate your children to clean their rooms — because you like clean rooms. You may want to motivate your spouse to take more time off work — because you want to spend more time with him or her. These are not their reasons. They are yours!

Motivation comes from external stimulus. It stems from the regressive lower levels of consciousness: hopelessness, sadness, shame, guilt, grief, fear, doubt, and anger and all are associated with external influences for action. You attempt to motivate when you try to shame someone into changing their behavior for your reasons. You attempt to motivate when you provoke guilt, fear, and doubt to get someone to do the things you want them to do. You may even try to motivate yourself through thoughts of shame or guilt or fear. "I have to pass this exam or my folks will be furious;" "I have to quit smoking or I will die of lung cancer." We know fear tactics in advertising or trying to motivate people to change their lifestyle through guilt, fear, shame rarely work for the long term. Nor does it lead to the inspired thought we are aiming for to attract success.

Inspiration is "inner directed" and involves taking action for personal reasons. Transcending consciousness can only be done by people for their own reasons — it is an inspired or "in spirit" state. Someone else may provide some fuel to your inspiration, but true inspiration comes from within for real and long-lasting change to occur. When my nephew, who is an outstanding personal trainer, said to me, "Auntie if you were to work out in the gym for three months you would see a huge difference," I was inspired. He gave me hope. I wanted to do it and he believed I could succeed. Weight loss has been a challenge for me, but I began to experience success following his encouragement. I continue with my intention for a healthy, vibrant body. When I feel inspired and hopeful and I hear his encouraging words, I am able to get my dream back on track knowing this dream, like many others I have had, is in the process of being fulfilled. I keep my consciousness at high levels, not blaming myself or feeling shame for my lack of progress.

When you are inspired, or when someone acts in a way to inspire you, it is you who first had the dream. Then others saw something you really wanted, and they were there to encourage you to keep the dream alive.

Inspiration arises from the emotions on the progressive side of the Body Conscious guide, both for the person who becomes inspired and for the individual who inspires. All empowering levels — gratitude, acceptance, empathy, love, joy, wonder, inner peace, bliss, and enlightenment — are associated with inspired thought. It comes from an awakening inside you. It comes from an inspired (in spirit) place.

You are inspired when you engage in activities to fulfill your intentions or dreams. You are passionate. You can work at it all day long and not tire because you see that your dream is manifesting. You may also be inspired just by observing or working alongside others who live their lives vibrating at these high levels of consciousness. Can you think of people you love to be around because they make you feel so good just by being in their presence?

If you want to be the inspiration in someone's life, you will be that inspiration only if you, too, are vibrating at high levels of consciousness. Did you have a particular teacher who really inspired you? What levels of consciousness do you recall they were vibrating at? They likely did not live their personal lives in vibrations of fear, intimidation, shame, or any of the low level vibrations — nor were their interactions with you based on these levels of emotion!

Always ask, "How do I inspire myself?" and "How can I be inspiring to others?" You will find your shift in thinking moves you into higher consciousness. This shift activates the personal responsibility necessary for you to become the person you want to be. You find when you approach others with emotions on the progressive side of consciousness, you truly are an inspiration to them. You give them a rare gift.

Pause and ask yourself, "How can I act in a way that will

inspire?" When you can do that, your relationships — at work, at home, or in your community — become truly abundant ones! Daily check your emotional barometer on the Body Conscious guide. Where are you today? Where are your family members? Are you a motivating factor — or an inspiring factor — for yourself and others?

31

Surrender

Factor Four

A fourth way to transcend levels of consciousness is to release, just let go, and learn to truly forgive with a sense of gratitude for what you have learned. In all stressful situations, it is resistance that creates stress, pain, and frustration. And the problem with resistance is, as Carl Jung said, "That which is resisted, persists."

You hurt only yourself by hanging on to the pain, physical or emotional. It will persist, bringing you down to levels of consciousness that attract and ensure an on-going experience of pain.

I had some business relationships that resulted in negative outcomes with people I thought were trusted friends. It was only when I appreciated how the experience enabled me to move in a totally new direction was I able to be grateful. I realized these people came into my life at a time to provide me an opportunity to make a change, if I chose to do so. Without this experience, I would not have moved on to some very fulfilling new activities. Once I realized the value of what I had previously perceived as negative, I was able to feel grateful for the "gift" they had given me. Are you open to looking for the gift in adversity?

I have been asked with some level of sarcasm if this means that people who master this Law of Attraction stuff are just happy all the time. Obviously not. It is from the low points in our lives we gain the insights to take things to higher levels. We express gratitude for those low moments because of the teachings they provide.

If you are feeling anxiety because you have financial challenges, you learn to release the feeling, let it go, or just flow with it. If you are grieving for someone, flow with it. Let it take its course. Be the Observer and do not resist against it. Can you feel calm in the midst of an intense emotion? Can you still hold a high vibration in the midst of grief?

Of course, you can. You feel the grief, you flow with it but you focus on the positive aspects of the experience. You hold the high vibration while you ride the flow of the low vibrational experience. The low vibration does not suck you under. It does not snuff your life energy. You feel it, while you aim to soar above it.

Recently, I had the pleasure of having a mother and her 30-some-year-old son attend one of my Attracting Success seminars. They told me of her father (his grandfather) who had recently passed on at the age of 85. He was a Conscious Attractor, a highly successful businessman, who owned a company ranked second in its industry in the US. They talked about how he was always calm, setting the tone for others around him. Just months after the death of his wife and following his own diagnosis of Parkinson's disease, he was called off the golf course to be informed his only son had been killed in an airplane crash. He gently took the hands of the pastor and his daughter, who were present for the giving of this news, and said, "Lord, let me live long enough to see the good this situation will bring."

This was just one example they shared of a man who attracted good things into his life by constantly vibrating at a level of gratitude, love, and joy. Regardless of what happened in his personal life or in his business life, he remained in non-duality, not resisting the emotion, but not letting the negative emotion rule him. He flowed with the emotion, seeking to regain his balance in a higher level vibration and always looking for the good in everything life presented him. When this gentleman was asked, "How did you do it?" he would reply, "I don't know…it is a gift."

To some, it is a gift. But the beauty of the study of the Law of Attraction is the gift is now being analyzed and broken into component parts, so it can be taught. Each of us can acquire the benefits of this style of living. It is a science. Wallace Wattles knew that almost 100 years ago when he wrote *The Science of Getting Rich*: "Man can form things in his thought and by impressing his thought upon formless substance, can cause the thing he thinks about to be created."

When you start to think in these new ways about the things that happen to you, you may find you no longer have as strong a connection with the friends or business associates you once had. Your new consciousness attracts different people and those who were attracted to you in the past will now find reason to be elsewhere. This may, at times, be hard to accept. You may still find many qualities about these people you respect and admire, but you tend to find yourself absorbed with new people who are more aligned with where you are now in your life. Embrace this as a good thing! You can't change while still hanging on to the past. Some relationships were only meant to last for a short time, while others will sustain us for a lifetime. Surrendering some relationships to be able to move forward may be a necessary step in your process.

32

New energy

Factor Five

A fifth factor in opening channels to higher vibrations is *removing clutter from your physical and mental spaces*, creating a void for new energy, ideas, and experiences to enter. Let go of the physical and mental things from your past that are blocking the path to your future. Most importantly, examine why you have created this cluttered, overcrowded energy in the first place. Look within yourself and ask profound questions: "Am I avoiding looking at my reality? Is this about feeling a sense of hopelessness and lack of control? Am I overwhelmed? Why am I choosing to create energy blocks?"

Ancient Eastern philosophies have detailed guidance on how to do this in your physical space through Chinese Feng Shui or East Indian Sthapatya Veda. You may study and apply these teachings or you may come to your own realization the clutter in your life is blocking your energy, lowering your vibration, and it just has to go! Your physical space is a vibrational extension of you. What is it saying? By cleaning this space, you create an opening for new and enriching energies to flow. Do you need all these material things? Are they a substitute for something else that is lacking? Everything has energy. If your physical space is blocked with the energy emanating from clutter there is no room for your creative energy to expand.

Our Western society, stripped of a connection to spirituality because of a preoccupation with the old scientific model, has replaced the emptiness created in that spiritual vacuum with external expressions of happiness. We are inundated with advertising telling us we will be more satisfied if we only possess more things. But these external objects have failed to fill the void. External things and experiences can bring us great pleasure but only when we first are in a place of inner peace and gratitude.

Not only do your physical closets and clutter require airing out, so too do your mental closets! You create space to take on new and higher levels of consciousness. Get rid of mental clutter! It is like the hard drive on your computer. You have limited memory and to bring in new and better programs, you need to remove some of the old ones.

Be alert to any second-hand thoughts that have taken on a "locked and upright" position in your mind! Only by carefully selecting the thoughts that align with who you really want to be, do you free up space for more positive thoughts to enter.

Mental clutter can also arise from surrounding yourself with negative people whose energies are diminishing yours. Why are you attracting these people into your life and why are you choosing to allow them to remain there if they do not uplift and inspire you?

Meditation is one way to clean your mental closets. By making this part of your daily routine, within just a few short weeks, there will be a calm energy surrounding you and the tendency to fluctuating moods or desires will be lessened. Deciding to change your thoughts or your circumstance also releases blocked mental energy and allows a conduit for new and refreshing levels of consciousness.

This purging of both physical and mental clutter is a lifelong routine to greatly enhance your quality of life. It lightens and liberates you to move to higher consciousness. Another way to heighten your consciousness is found in your choice of day-to-day activities.

33

Good vibes

Factor Six

Our sixth path to higher consciousness is our choice of life experiences. Some experiences give us uplifting vibrations filling our vessels to overflowing, while others seem to drag us down and deplete our energy. Read the first list slowly, paying attention to how your body feels. Experience the energy of each word and sense where you are experiencing this in your body.

Life experiences that lower my vibration:
> Violence — in reality or in movies or television programs
> Heavy metal music
> Obnoxious and negative people
> Addictive substances (alcohol, tobacco, drugs)
> Congestion — traffic, communities
> Judging and making negative comments about others
> Foul language
> Overloaded with activities and expectations
> Exercising to excess
> Consistent loud noises
> Overcrowded living spaces
> Lack of forgiveness
> Dishonesty with self and others
> Excessive workloads and tight deadlines

Now, take a deep breath. You may want to shift your gaze to a beautiful picture, a favorite object, a person in the room, or look outdoors at a lovely landscape for a moment to neutralize the energy you have just experienced. Consider how your body is feeling. Write down your feelings.

Now read the second list slowly, noticing the feelings it generates just from just hearing the words.

Life experiences that raise my vibration:
> Doing kind deeds
> Meditation
> Play-fullness
> Attitudes of celebration/gratitude/spirituality
> Journal writing
> Soothing music
> Soft lighting/candles/esthetically pleasing surroundings
> Walks in nature
> Running water or water fountains in your home
> Art/beauty appreciation
> Pleasing conversations with friends/family
> Uplifting books and movies
> Healthy foods and beverages
> Staying in the moment
> Appropriate exercise
> Creative pursuits

I expect most, if not all of you, had a sense of sadness, doom, or a sickening feeling in the pit of your stomach reading the words on the first list.

I expect the second list felt light, uplifting, calming, and energizing. Can you imagine being able to hold a high level of consciousness if most of your experiences were those on the first list? It just is not possible, is it? And yet, many people in Western society live a daily diet of those experiences, especially vulnerable and impressionable children.

Imagine. If you feel a different vibration just by reading the words — what impact will it have on you to be living these experiences! We have all felt the heavy, unhappy feeling the low vibration list can give us and in contrast, the uplifting feeling of the high vibration list. The activities on each list individually may not be enough to make a significant difference but the more optimal experiences we bring into our lives, the more we notice a shift in consciousness.

Living high vibrational life experiences generates a sense of calm. If you are living your life in an environment as described by the second list, it is unlikely you have attitudes of dualistic, judgmental thinking. You are less likely to experience high levels of stress or be a victim of burnout. Instead your life unfolds with a quiet calmness and serenity. You are open and tolerant of others ideas and beliefs.

To transcend to higher consciousness, make it a daily habit to experience life from the second list. Dr. William Braud has an interesting quote that reflects these two opposing levels of consciousness:

> It appeared that people were operating on two planes, the hard, striving, motivated plane of the world or the relaxed, positive, receptive world of the Field and the two seemed incompatible.

The Body Conscious guide parallels Braud's contrasting planes. The regressive, dualistic emotional plane is contrasted with the progressive, non-dualistic plane of higher consciousness. You cannot access the higher planes while holding on to the regressive emotions of duality. Many of the things on our first list of life experiences represent the hard, striving, motivated plane of the world. The second list of life experiences represents the

relaxed, positive, receptive world of the Field. Braud is absolute-
ly correct. They are incompatible. Decide where you want to live
your life. You cannot access the abundance of your intuitive, creative genius that resides in the universal energy field, if you are
coming from low level vibrations, or as Braud refers to it, "the
hard, striving, motivated plane of the world."

Simply put, the Law of Attraction will not work to bring positive
things into your life if you are vibrating or living in low levels of
consciousness. Change your vibration, your emotional energy,
and celebrate a life lived in high vibrational experiences.

34

Celebration

Factor Seven

The seventh and last suggestion for raising your levels of consciousness is to find reason to celebrate all that is right in your life. Choose to start each day by examining what there is to celebrate, right now. Celebrate every small movement towards your ideal. Regardless of how difficult your life may seem at the moment, you can take baby steps and celebrate any movement in the right direction. Here is the chance to exercise your free will. Every situation has its negatives and its positives. You choose where you focus your attention.

This traditional First Nations story "Two Wolves" speaks to your free will to choose.

> An elderly Cherokee Native American was teaching his grandchildren about life.
>
> He said to them, "A fight is going on inside me; it is a terrible fight and it is between two wolves. One wolf is evil — he is fear, anger, envy, sorrow, regret, greed, arrogance, self-pity, guilt, resentment, inferiority, lies, false pride, competition, superiority, and ego.
>
> "The other is good — he is joy, peace, love, hope, sharing, serenity, humility, kindness, benevolence, friendship, empathy, generosity, truth, compassion, and faith.

"This same fight is going on inside you, and inside every other person, too."

They thought about it for a minute, and then one child asked his grandfather, "Which wolf will win, Grandfather?"

The elder simply replied, "The one you feed."

Which wolf do you want to feed? Who will thrive? What do you choose to focus on and celebrate?

Go about your day finding reasons to celebrate — found money, a call from a dear friend, a compliment or a smile from a stranger. Be grateful and celebrate all that is happening in your life right now — right at this moment. Resist the temptation to say, "I will be happy when..." This celebration approach to life raises your vibration and quickly allows you to be in a receiving mode for even greater things. Celebrate what is right for you. Be grateful, and from this place of gratitude you allow more wonderful things to appear.

> Your Fourth Insight. The dream, in the process of unfolding, holds the vibration that is success, fulfillment, and true happiness. Always hold a dream.

Getting started

Personal change involves becoming informed, then integrating the new ideas and behaviors into your daily routine, and finally, internalizing them so they are who you have BECOME. It is all about you BEING MORE!

Purchase a celebration journal and begin today writing for five minutes all the things you have to celebrate.

What is your dominant vibration? Is it serving you? Where would you aspire to be vibrating on the Body Conscious guide?

What are your thoughts in the areas of your life where you would like to see different results? Do you see a match between those thoughts and your current results?

Create a channel changer to block old voices and messages you no longer want to hear.

For one evening select at least five items from the positive life experiences list and incorporate them into your evening. Invite a friend. How did it make you feel? You may want to make this a weekly event!

Use the Body Conscious guide to prompt meaningful conversations with friends and family members. Ask each other, "How did 'that' (experience, word, thought) make you feel? How are you feeling (emotionally) today?"

Ask your family members and friends, "How may I inspire you?"

Be the inspiration in someone's life today!

Summary
<u>HAVE</u>
Transcending Consciousness

Thought triggers a feeling, and the feeling gives off a vibration. The universal energy field connects with the frequency of that vibration, returning back more of what we vibrate.

Being a Conscious Attractor starts with having a clear and strong intention for what we want.

Hold a vibration in harmony or in support of what you desire to manifest.

The Body Conscious guide makes it clear which energies are empowering to the individual and humankind and which are disempowering, which are regressive and which are progressive.

Low level vibrations attract low level experiences while the high levels of consciousness are necessary to attract the life experiences you prefer.

The turning point from disempowerment to empowerment, from duality to non-duality, from regressive to progressive is gratitude.

After expressing gratitude one seeks to live in non-duality, devoid of judgmental, dualistic thinking.

To attract higher experiences and abundance in our lives, we vibrate at the progressive levels of consciousness of non-duality.

Clean out your physical and mental clutter. Meditate.

Flow with emotion, letting go of low level vibrations and moving toward increasingly higher levels by being alert to the good in every experience.

<u>DO</u>
Intuition

The Intuitive Mind
is a sacred gift
And the rational mind
Is a faithful servant.

We have created a society
That honors the servant
And has forgotten the gift.
– Albert Einstein

35

"In spirit" actions

Inspiration, "in spirit" action, or intuition — the last leg of your journey to making your dreams a reality!

Are you feeling ready to create an exciting new future? Are you energized and ready to accept nothing less than 100% commitment to making it happen? Can you trust your ability to create the world as you wish to see it?

Reflect for a moment on what you already have to celebrate. Keep track of the personal changes or insights you are experiencing. Some of them may seem small, but major changes are nothing more than an accumulation of small things.

You express gratitude for waking up in a free country. You might record that in your Gratitude journal. Then, in your Celebration journal, take time daily to write about your experiences from the perspective of "What's here to celebrate?" This preference to see the good in all things becomes the normal way of thinking for you, the Conscious Attractor.

With your increased knowledge of the science behind the Law of Attraction, you are now amongst a growing number of people aware of a spiritual awakening that is the essence and purpose for living this law. Spiritual awakening transcends religious denomination and unites us in our common quest for Higher Self, purpose and meaning.

You now know how to create conscious intention — the BE step in our process. You also understand your results are related to the emotional vibration you hold — the HAVE step. You have access to a guide, the Body Conscious, to show you a path to ever higher levels of consciousness and the separation of dualistic and non-dualistic thinking.

In the three-step process, the final step is DO — inspired, intuitive action. Typically, in our action-oriented society we first focus on "What do I have to DO!" when we want to solve a problem or change a circumstance. A problem presents itself, and we get busy with DOING solutions. To decide on what we will DO, we often replay solutions from past experiences and are surprised when we keep getting more of the same.

Rarely will you find genius or creativity in a linear action plan. We also tend to plan only as big as we know we can accomplish. This plan lacks magic or creative spark and most often contains mechanistic, left-brain solutions. If we want to take a vacation, we plan an itinerary to fit the size of budget we think we can put together rather than dreaming of what we want and allowing inspiration and intuition to lead the way.

The type of doing we talk about requires trusting that a solution much greater than anything you can plan for will appear. This "in spirit," intuitive doing allows for magnificent synchronicities and coincidences to bring rich abundant solutions. You imagine what you want and hold on to the belief that a way, an action, or a plan will be shown to you. If your dream vacation is to travel the world for one year, hold on to the dream. You will be amazed at the opportunities that appear from places you are not even aware of yet.

I have heard students of the Law of Attraction say, "You just need to put it out there and it will materialize. Turn it over to the universe." That statement implies that one has no power or responsibility in the process. All you have to do is to ASK, and then sit, and wait to receive. It is true that you ask and it is given, but you must also do something.

As Einstein said, "Every vibration you offer creates your future. Everything in the universe is a movement of energy. Nothing happens until something moves."

You act from inspiration. This story always reminds me to listen to the voice of our Higher Self or intuition. It always speaks. But if you are not listening or if you have a preconceived idea of the way in which it will speak, you may truly "miss the boat."

> A man is stranded on the rooftop of his house during a flood. The waters are rapidly rising, and the man is praying to God to save him. Soon another man paddles up to him in a canoe and says, "Jump in, I have room!" To which the stranded gentleman says, "No, I'm fine. God is going to save me." Next a motorboat comes along and the dialogue is repeated. The man on the roof insists he is waiting for God. A sailboat and a yacht appear, and again, he refuses. Finally, the water has reached his chin. He tilts his head upwards and rants at the sky, "God, where are you? I thought you were going to save me." A loud voice rumbles out of the dark clouds saying, "Well, I sent you a canoe...a motorboat...a sailboat!"

Trust the solutions will be brought to you and these solutions will be more exciting and rewarding than your logical mind could ever have conceived. There is abundant genius residing in the thought processes of the energy field. You experience "Eureka" solutions. When you hear your intuitive voice, don't hesitate to take action. The Law of Attraction delivers, but you participate by being open and listening. Your guidance comes from your sixth and often most underdeveloped sense, your sense of intuition.

36

Our sixth sense

Trust your hunches. They're usually based on facts filed away just below the conscious level.
  – Dr. Joyce Brothers

In our science-based world, we focus on our five physical senses — touch, taste, smell, sight, and hearing — relying on them to guide us in our daily activities. If you stick your finger into a flame, you quickly learn this is an unpleasant or painful experience, and you trust that all other flames will give the same results. This experience guides future actions and reinforces trust in important sensory message systems.

We have another sense. It is likely our most important but, sadly, almost ignored sense. It is that little inner voice, the vibrational language of the universe. It may not actually be a voice as you normally think of voices. It speaks in feelings and visualizations, in pictures or symbols. It speaks to us in dreams. It speaks creatively, unfolding, leaving us in awe of the process! It is the voice of imagination and genius. It is our sixth and most important sense — our intuition or emotional guidance system.

This sense may be more finely developed in people whose inclination is toward more right-brain or creative thinking. That may be one reason it tends to be ignored in a left-brain dominant, power-based society. It holds little credibility in the scientific world, a world relying heavily on scientific method. Developing and trusting your intuition is integral to living in the Law of Attraction.

There may be fear underlying the reluctance to develop our sixth sense — a fear coming from "secondhand" thoughts about possible "psychic implications." After all, they killed the "witches," didn't they! Or some people may fear they could hear or tune into something they don't want to hear or tune in to. Or they may think exploring intuition is in conflict with their religious beliefs.

Not listening to your intuition is a lot like ignoring the messages your eyes are sending when you are about to step off a high cliff! Doesn't it seem a little absurd to ignore a message from your sixth sense when you look at it that way! You were given six senses to guide you, why wouldn't you want to take full advantage of all of them?

Science-based culture is almost totally reliant upon the five physical senses but the sixth sense, our intuitive sense, is equally powerful and credible. Not using your intuitive sense to guide you in a world awakened to consciousness is like being sightless in a physical world. It is the connection to the universal field of consciousness where all knowledge, creativity, and wisdom can be found, yet, you may be saying, "I don't want to know what lies there!"

Society has been so bombarded with the noise of media, spoken word, and written word, that it is at risk of total disconnect from the inner intuitive communication. Minimizing external racket, being quiet, meditating, getting in tune with nature, all serve to reawaken this vital gift. In a state of quietness, an idea comes to you. An opportunity presents itself. A call is made. Someone rings your doorbell. You feel the need to go to the store, and you act on it. When you get there, you meet someone perfectly positioned to provide the information or contacts you were seeking.

Be alert to intuitive nudges from the universe. Act on those nudges. Sometimes the reason for the nudge is immediately apparent. Other times you may think, "Well, that was a wild goose chase. There was nothing there for me." Trust and have faith. The reason may be temporarily hidden from you. Be open — accept — act, and wait for the reasons to be revealed!

Accessing the rich, creative source of solutions through our intuition, our emotional guidance system, or our sixth sense, is a mode of thinking essential for survival in our rapidly advancing quantum world.

We have many words for intuition: hunches, still voices, premonitions, just a sense. Sometimes it is confusing as to whether you are hearing your intuitive voice or whether these messages are coming from the external world. Are they possibly my own desires to control the situation or am I really hearing my intuitive voice? Learning to tell the difference requires patience and practice.

First, you summon original thoughts. The less crowded your mind is with "locked-in" thinking the more room you have in your "database" to receive new messages. Begin today by protecting yourself against secondhand thoughts. Ask frequently, "Is this really what I want to think? What do I want to believe? Is this even true? Is this thought so strong it is preventing me from being open to opposing or different opinions?"

This discipline assists you in separating the chatter of the world from your small, inner, intuitive voice so it can be heard. The inner voice will rarely yell! The only way you hear is when you slow down, become quiet, clear out loud and obnoxious chatter in your brain, and LISTEN. Whenever you get a vibration or hear a little voice or get a sense of someone calling, pay attention and follow up with action.

I was mentoring a woman who, at a very low point in the process, plopped herself onto the sofa and said, "I give up. It should not be this difficult. Why can't I make this business succeed?" Almost instantly, she heard an inner voice telling her to call the chairman of the hospital foundation and propose a meeting to talk about a partnership. She recognized this might be the intuitive voice we had been talking about and immediately leapt up to make the call. The chairman asked, "When could she meet with him in his office?" He held back the print on a brochure pending the results of their meeting. Within 40 minutes, she was in his office, a partnership was formed, and she was on the brochure! Forty-five minutes of hesitation and she would have missed the opportunity!

Later, some of her marketing colleagues told me they had had a similar thought about contacting the hospital but had not followed through with the action!

She had a strong FEELING and acted on it.

Your intuition is often experienced as a feeling.

Recognize the feelings and honor them. Then enter into dialogue with your inner voice. Ask for feedback. Check each decision, however small, as a way of developing your communication skills through your feelings and inner voice.

"Should I take this journey?"

Wait and listen to the voice or feeling that comes with the question.

"Should I take this journey today?"

Wait and listen again for the feeling or voice. Is there a difference?

As soon as you realize you are arguing and debating, questioning whether this is an intuitive thought or an ego thought — or if you are struggling to decide what you need to do, unable to give up control — you can assume you are out of heart (intuition), and into head (logic). You experience an unsettled or uncomfortable feeling.

I was scheduled to do a course in Pennsylvania when about mid-week, I began to get calls from the facilitator concerned about registration, road conditions, and fretting that perhaps we should cancel. I encouraged her to pause, go within, and ask, "What am I feeling?" She immediately responded that her intuitive feeling was to go ahead. It would all work out. Despite the flurry of emails and telephones calls preceding this conversation, she intuitively knew this, but her head was getting in the way. If there is a flurry, you know you are in the head, using logic and debate. Once she trusted her intuition, she knew what she was being directed to do. We went ahead and because our numbers were small, we were able to hear stories we would otherwise not have heard in a large group, one of which has made it into this book!

Begin to talk to your inner voice as you would another person. Ask many questions and test your emotional response to the answers. It may, at times, seem challenging to know if it is your head voice or your intuitive voice doing the talking! First, know the head voice often links to ego, and the ego may be linked to low vibrations of fear, doubt, and scarcity. If what you think you are listening to is bringing up some of those low level vibrations, you know you are in your head or ego. If you are rationalizing, plotting, planning, arguing, you are also in your head. The intuitive voice is a quiet KNOWING — still, deep, calm — learn to trust it!

37

Tap into intuition

If we have disconnected from intuition or if we give it little credibility, we are in essence handicapping ourselves. It is a lot like gradually losing your sense of sight. Following are two techniques you can use to tap into your intuition. The techniques are applied kinesiology and the ancient art of dowsing. They are fun to explore as you develop and learn to trust your intuitive guidance system.

Applied Kinesiology

Drs. Goodhart and Diamond. In the 1960s and 70s, Drs. George Goodhart and John Diamond developed a system of muscle testing called applied kinesiology. Dr. Goodhart believed, since all organs of the body were attached to a muscle, if the organ was in an unhealthy state, the strength of the muscle would be compromised. He found the body tested weak when unhealthful physical stimuli came in contact with the individual, and strong in the presence of healthful stimuli.

In the 70s, Dr. Diamond, intrigued by the work of Dr. Goodhart, explored similar testing for emotional and intellectual stimuli with equally fascinating results. The body seemed to test strong in a supportive and loving environment and weak in negative environments. If you smile at someone, even at the back of their head, and conduct the muscle test, they test strong. Should you think negative thoughts about the individual, even standing out of their line of sight, they test weak.

Imagine the implications of this on a daily basis as we allow our-selves to be bombarded by negative influences — television pro-grams, violent movies, traffic congestion, negative people, and so on. Our bodies are recording and reacting to each and every neg-ative influence, weakening our resolve and depleting our energy stores.

Dr. David R. Hawkins. Hawkins is a psychiatrist, medical researcher, and author. His books, *Power vs Force, Truth vs Falsehood* and *Transcending Consciousness* describe his research on consciousness using applied kinesiology. He con-tends applied kinesiology, or muscle testing, is the body's com-munication with the truth residing in the universal energy field.

At a cellular level, it seems there is an intelligence longing to communicate with us if we master the technique. Applied kine-siology is a method of using the body as a truth compass or cos-mic polygraph. Dr. Hawkins states, "Applied kinesiology exposed for the first time, the intimate connection between mind and body revealing the mind 'thinks' with the body itself."

Is it possible our mind resides in every living cell of the body? Hawkins refers to this connection of mind/body and universal energy field as "a form of communal consciousness — a database of consciousness." He describes applied kinesiology in this way: "Muscle testing is the wormhole between two universes — the physical, and the mind and spirit — an interface between two dimensions."

He likens the discovery of the use of applied kinesiology for assessing truth and knowledge to the discovery of the lodestone. Finding the first magnetic rocks may not have seemed like a huge discovery, but once people realized the potential of these unusual stones as a compass, it opened the doors to great discoveries. Likewise, using the techniques of applied kinesiology to access universal truth and knowledge is as profound as the application of a magnetic stone to a compass.

In Appendix A, the method of doing applied kinesiology is described. Practice the technique through the recommended exercises and then use it to test the truth of the intention statement that you prepared in the section on "BE – Intention," and your channel changer developed in the segment "HAVE – Transcending Consciousness."

When doing applied kinesiology tests, your results may be skewed if one of the partners is tired, ill or is at an emotionally low vibration. I once invited two people to come to the front of the room to demonstrate this technique. All of the basic tests we conducted were giving completely opposite results to what I expected. After the course was over someone confided in me these two people did not get along at all! I obviously had encountered some very low level vibrations! I have since learned to let participants choose their own partners!

John Diamond says,

> While no one can have positive thoughts and attitudes all of the time, everyone can have them most of the time. Once we have been convinced by Applied Kinesiology that hateful and destructive thoughts can deplete our life energy (while loving and nurturing thoughts can increase it) the decision is ours as to which path to take.

Role of the thymus gland

The thymus gland in adults has been an intriguing study, with theories that it has no role, to more recent studies over the past twenty years suggesting it is the link between mind and body. The word "thymos" is Greek and means "life force" or "soul." In ancient times, it was thought to be the controller of the body's life energies.

Starting from puberty, the thymus gland shrinks in size. It is particularly affected by stress, causing it to shrink even more. You may get incorrect readings while working with someone whose thymus is testing very weak. In Appendix A you will find some tips on how to revitalize your thymus gland prior to doing applied kinesiology testing.

The ancient art of the pendulum

Communicating with the inner self or higher consciousness can also be accessed by the ancient art of the pendulum, called dowsing. This is one of the easiest and most convenient ways to tap into intuition. It is merely another way of confirming what we probably already know at an intuitive level.

Anyone can learn to use the pendulum. Some adults may take time to get it working due to difficulties in letting go and learning to trust. You note that trust and surrender are always important in the work we do with the Law of Attraction. Playing with your pendulum awakens your ability to trust and surrender.

One of Britain's best-known medical dowers, the late Bruce MacManaway, once claimed,

> Dowsing seems to be able to form a bridge for bringing to the conscious understanding of the intellect factors that are known in the subconscious. In the case of healing, the factors are probably known in the subconscious of both the patient and the healer but some mechanism is needed to reach them.

The pendulum is a weight attached to a cord. The weight is typically a crystal or semi-precious stone on a chain, but that is not necessary. One of the world's greatest dowsers, Tom Lethbridge, once used a piece of chewing gum at the end of a string! A pendulum can be any weighted object at the end of a length of string or chain.

When you begin to use your pendulum, whatever form it might take, you begin by setting up the way in which it responds to "Yes," "No," and "Ask again" statements. Here is how one frequent user of the pendulum describes the experience:

> Many years ago I discovered dowsing as a wonderful way to give me a visual connection to my intuition. What was it my body really wanted or needed? Finding that out was one of my primary reasons for wanting to acquire this skill. My holistic nursing consultant was using this technique to identify my nutritional needs at the physical, mental and spiritual levels. When she offered a course I jumped at the chance. Dowsing looked so easy that I was surprised when my pendulum didn't start moving until four months after the course was completed! I guess it is about when the student is ready! I have also since learned that dehydration and chaos in our lives can block our energy flow and affect the movement of the pendulum. My pendulum has totally opposite movements for yes and no than what is typical. That tells me it is my pendulum's personality because it consistently gives me these responses! I now carry the pendulum in my pocket and use it daily to verify my "intuitive sense of things!"

Dowsing with a pendulum can be done to get answers to the same questions you would use for muscle testing. You may want to use both applied kinesiology and the pendulum to confirm your results. The one advantage of the pendulum is that it can be used to check intuition when you are alone.

Today the pendulum is used by the military, oil companies, and spiritual healers to detect anything from electromagnetic fault lines to health problems. If you decide to pursue pendulum dowsing, you can also test your intention statement and compare the results to those you obtained from the applied kinesiology or muscle testing.

Professor Hans-Dieter Betz, an expert on dowsing, says this:

> I am now inclined to believe that the mechanism of dowsing is on some kind of a continuum which starts with electro-magnetism, but ends with something we don't yet understand — an ability of the human consciousness to somehow access hidden information. It is beyond me as a physicist to explain it.

Whatever it is the pendulum is acting as a sender and receiver of, I think we can assume it is somehow through telekinesis, connecting with the subconscious or intuitive voice.

Hydration

Whether you are using applied kinesiology or the pendulum, it is essential the body is well hydrated. Just as you would not consider heading off on a journey without making certain you had sufficient gas, so too, will you want to make certain you check your body's fuel system, which is water. Our bodies are 75% water. The brain and other specific organs are at even higher percentages.

Here is a tip. Ask your pendulum if you are well hydrated. If the answer is no, ask how many glasses of water you need to drink to be sufficiently hydrated to proceed with your testing! And also, test your choice of water sources with the pendulum or with applied kinesiology!

These techniques are means by which you can learn to trust your intuitive voice. When you have a thought about something and you are not sure if it is the right thing for you, use applied kinesiology or the pendulum to affirm or deny your intuitive conclusions.

38

Wisdom through dreams

The awake state may be essentially the same as the dreaming state, only partially anchored by external stimuli. In this view, your conscious life is an awake dream.
  – David Easleman, 10 Unsolved Mysteries of the Brain

Dreams are another way our intuition may be attempting to communicate with us and can be a source of guidance to inspired actions. In dream research it appears much of brain activity is similar to that of the waking state. It could be said then that your conscious life is nothing more than an "awake dream." Or that a dream is a "conscious life" with your eyes closed! In ancient civilizations, great attention was paid to dreams and to the meaning of dreams. Decisions by heads of state were made based on dreams. Families communicated with each other about the contents of their dreams. By the seventeenth and eighteenth centuries the western world moved into a scientific model, and attention to dreams was lost. When dream consciousness returned, it was through the work of Freud and Jung. Unfortunately as a result, much of current attitudes about dreams link their value only to psychotherapy and not to the day-to-day wisdom they are providing.

In this prophesized resurgence of spirituality and the movement to higher levels of consciousness, we should again see dreams resume their all-important role as part of our sixth sense wisdom. By reawakening intuition, we influence our ability to dream "daytime" dreams as well as nighttime dreams!

Isn't it interesting we use the word "dream" to refer to our intentions for a future time in our life, and also, to those nocturnal
"movies" playing each night! Many people in my seminars
stopped creating dreams for their future, and interestingly state
they are also unable to recall their nocturnal dreams. There is a
link.

It is good practice to write down your dreams and learn to translate them. What could these dream symbols possibly mean? Are
there some intuitive messages being ignored in daytime hours
that are being communicated again in a quieter state?

Your intuitive voice nudges you with important bits of information and wisdom, and when you ignore the voices during waking
hours, the messages continue to come through the symbolic language of dreams. That is why dream translation is critical to the
awakening of intuition. Perhaps you had a dream about a car
accident. Then you have one. You are now assuming you are
clairvoyant but you missed the point by taking a literal translation of the dream. Dream messages are usually more symbolic.
They guide you to a different course of action. In this instance,
the wisdom held in the dream may have been a message telling
you to slow down and take better care of yourself. The symbolism
of a car in a dream is often a representation of your physical
body. The crash in your dream is an indication you need to
change your lifestyle to avoid the harm you may be doing to your
body. The fact you ignored this message or did not understand
how to translate the symbolism, and happened to have an actual car accident does not mean that you have experienced precog-
nition. It could have been any number of events that could have
happened to get you to slow down. You may have had a serious
fall and suffered broken limbs. Or you may have come down with
an illness that has you bedridden for a long period of time. The
real dream message was that you were not taking adequate care

of yourself. Without understanding this symbolic language, you now recover from the accident but continue on with your lifestyle until another "stroke of bad luck" hits you. You have totally missed the wisdom being communicated to you.

Once you realize life is not something happening TO you, and instead that you are the one making life happen, you definitely want to develop this all-important skill of listening to the symbolic messages of your dreams enhancing your overall intuitive ability as a skill to design your life as you wish it to be.

39

Balancing brain hemispheres

Only the person who has freed himself of the dominance of the left brain hemisphere can allow himself and the world To BE.
  – Dr. Carl Johan Calleman

We have spent a lot of time pointing out this process of BECOM-ING, of BEING before DOING, of shifting to more right-brain thinking to become balanced in left- and right-brain hemi-spheres. It's about freeing ourselves of left-brain dominance. If you have been working with the Law of Attraction but wonder-ing why you are not getting the results you want, perhaps now you can appreciate the shift that needs to happen. It is a shift from doing to being, and from left-brain thinking (logical and lin-ear) to increased use of right-brain thinking (creative and intu-itive) — optimally balancing left and right brain hemispheres.

Engage in as many right-brain activities as possible to awaken this part of your mind. Mediation is the first and most important technique for balancing. Then paint, write, sing, draw, gaze at sunsets, plant flowers, doodle on your notebook, strum your gui-tar, read great literature, take breathtaking photos, or simply stroll through a beautiful park! Participate in these activities for the sheer joy they bring.

It doesn't matter if you are a professional artist — go ahead and paint! Anything worth doing is worth doing badly!

I was taught if you are going to do it, "You must excel." The implied message seemed to be "If you can't excel, don't bother doing it." But I now have a new perspective. If it gives you pleasure, if it gives you joy, just do it! Even if you are not good at it, it doesn't matter! It's okay to paint those "ugly" pictures just because you love to do it — without concern as to how others may rate your work. How liberating! How uplifting! How "non-dualistic!"

While engaging in something you love, you raise your vibration and all other aspects of your life unfold in a rich and abundant way! You do so without fear of judgment or evaluation!

Balancing both hemispheres and accessing creative energy provides a life experience that is not only enriching for you but also is a lot more FUN!

You recall the Mayan Nine Great Cycles chart developed by Dr. Calleman on page 58. Note the importance he places on right-brain development as an integral part of the evolution of consciousness. We have moved out of the Planetary Cycle of Power and are in the midst of the Eighth Great Cycle of Ethics and Spirituality. In this Cycle the shift is to right-brain development. Spiritual concepts and growth are reliant upon right-brain faculty.

Calleman has even stronger statements to make about the reasons why you should make a shift to more right-brain activity — reasons more serious than just having more fun. He says,

> Those who deny the change in consciousness that the divine process of creation now brings about — or actually imposes on us — and fails to develop their intuition accordingly, will sooner or later find themselves at a dead end.

> The world we are now entering...is fundamentally about
> healing, about creating balance both on a global and on
> an individual scale...it is about unifying the East and
> West....Trusting your intuition is really about trusting
> yourself, your whole being sometimes in the face of seem-
> ingly logical arguments of others and the constant chat-
> tering of your own mind.

A spiritual path is a creative journey. Remember, we use the word spiritual as "becoming one with your universe." Your choice of religion is just that, your choice. But we commonly seek a spiritual path. It is becoming attuned to who you are and your purpose. This journey has no end point. It is life-long.

Today science is so dominated by left-brain thinking that there is great difficulty getting acceptance for research on spirituality or even intuition. It is thought of as pseudoscience, not belonging in realm of academia. But Albert Einstein did not share that opinion. Einstein believed in a connection to a Higher Being. Perhaps that explains his amazing contributions!

The challenge is we live in a society where, as even Einstein recognized decades ago, we honor the rational mind and totally ignore the intuitive mind.

How can someone who has been educated and socialized in this western culture decide to make greater use of one's right-brain capabilities? Is it possible to change from the linear, pragmatic left-brain style of thinking and become more creative and spontaneous?

Well you can! We all can!

It starts with wanting to make a change. It starts with you having a light-bulb moment that things are not going all that well with your current approach. You stand up and declare you are ready for something new. It comes from going inside and asking yourself, "Is there something about what is being said here that resonates as truth with me? Have I experienced listening to my inner voice and found it to be good guidance?"

Life is about balance in all areas, and balancing your left (analytical, logical mind) and right hemispheres (creative, intuitive mind) brings you much closer to maximizing the full potential of the human brain.

40

Now, go DO!

Now, you should be ready to let go of trying to control everything, able to flow with the process, and well-prepared to implement the third step of the Law of Attraction process — DO inspired, "in spirit," intuitive actions!

Just be relaxed — open to possibility. Go about your life. Take a walk. Have fun. Trust the answers will come. It may be the last place you would ever have thought the solution would be found, but you know it is right when it delights you!

You may think you have a better way or a better solution. You may want to act quickly to put your solution to work. But being able to let go is about trusting how rich and creative inspired solutions can be. Study the works of great geniuses. They often say they accessed solutions in their sleep or in a relaxed state when they were not trying to figure it out. It just came to them.

Time and again you hear successful people giving credit to a higher source of consciousness for their accomplishments. They heard, they listened, and they acted. The important thing is to act when you have the feeling. I know from my own experiences coincidence and unusual things can happen when I act on my intuitive hunches. Like the time I found my angel pen.

I was to attend a personal development workshop with an associate when I received a call from his brother telling me he had a rare and life-threatening virus and was in critical care. His survival was questionable. I spent the entire morning sending loving and healing messages and thoughts for his well being.

During the break I had a strong impulse to go and purchase the book, *The Seven Spiritual Laws of Success* by Deepak Chopra. The impulse was directing me to have everyone in the class write a personal note of love to him in the book with prayers for his full recovery. The impulse was so strong. I knew I had to act.

I was able to find a bookstore and purchase the title. As I hurried back to the meeting room, I saw something bright and shiny on the floor. I bent down to pick it up and was instantly struck with a dramatic attack of goose bumps — ever had one of those? I mean the hair on the back of my neck felt like it truly was standing on end. This was a feeling I had never experienced to this magnitude. It is something I now jokingly call a cosmic goose. Perhaps hair standing on end is that universal energy shouting — communicating with us in the loudest way it can!

I picked up a little gold pen. It was topped with an angel. The pen was very shiny with no marks to suggest it had been used or had lain about for long time.

It was 10:30 in the morning, and oddly enough there was not one person in the area. I again had a feeling I was being guided to take the pen along with the book and have everyone in the class write a note. The message was strong — "No other pen could be used."

The urge to have this book signed with this pen ONLY was so overpowering, I was shaking when I returned to the seminar. My compassionate colleagues sensed the intensity of my emotion and proceeded to fill the book with words of encouragement.

My friend recovered, much to the amazement of his doctor, who told him that another patient with identical symptoms died shortly after arriving at hospital.

I learned something that day about intuition, about a universal energy voice, about the "inexplicable." Perhaps what I really learned was nothing more than if the little voice speaks, you must act. Often, we won't know why we are being prompted to do something by our inner voice. Maybe the action just takes us away from a place that had we stayed, we would have been in danger. Maybe something like the love that flowed through that little pen did have an impact on my friend's recovery. Some things we may never know.

> Your Fifth Insight When you "hear" or "feel" the little inner voice of your intuition, act in an "in spirit" way.

Intuition is a soft, quiet voice that cannot be heard over the din of the television, crowded streets, garbage trucks, or sirens. Living a tranquil life puts you in better earshot of your inner voice. Listen and trust and DO — in spirit actions.

Getting started

Personal change involves becoming informed, then integrating the new ideas and behaviors into your daily routine, and finally, internalizing them so they are who you have BECOME. It is all about you BEING MORE!

Consider an area of your life where you want different results and carefully assess what you have been thinking. What is your inner voice telling you? Have you been listening? Has it been telling you to slow down? Get more exercise? Contact a friend?

Pay attention to your dreams for at least one week. Leave a notepad by your bed and write down whatever dreams you can recall in the morning. Think about the symbolism of the dream. If this was your intuitive voice talking to you in the daytime, what might it be saying? The dream is not literal. It is a symbolic message about your life.

Frequently ask yourself, "How is this making me FEEL?" Learn to label the feelings. Get more competent at trusting them and acting on what your feelings are telling you. It is the feeling that attracts in the Law of Attraction. Whatever you are feeling is what you get more of!

Engage in right-brain activities to stimulate your right hemisphere. Draw with your left hand. Take some beautiful photos. Tour an art gallery.

Practice using applied kinesiology. Test your name. Test

physical items such as fruit or sugar. Test emotional responses. Test your water supply. Test your intention statements. Test your channel changer.

Make or purchase a pendulum and have fun testing for "Yes" or "No" responses. Use your pendulum to verify the results you are receiving with applied kinesiology, especially with your intention statement.

Keep your body well hydrated when doing work with your intention.

Trust your feelings to guide your intuitive hunches toward "in spirit" actions.

Share your experiences. Your stories bring hope and inspiration to others.

Summary
<u>DO</u>
Intuition

Inspired doing comes from a connection with intuition.

Intuition is the vibrational voice of the universe.

Intuition is imagination and right-brain creativity.

To DO "in spirit actions," we must free ourselves of the dominance of left-brain thinking.

The next step in consciousness evolution is the connection with our intuition.

Intuition is learning to trust ourselves.

BE STILL to hear your quiet inner voice.

Think original thoughts.

Get your ego and persona out of the way.

Applied kinesiology and pendulum dowsing enable you to communicate with the universal field to determine truth.

The thymus is your life force or center. Use the thymus thump if you are feeling energy depleted.

Your journey starts now!

If people became aware that a power over another human being was impossible because of quantum physics, the world would be a different place for all of us. Quantum mechanics, perhaps more clearly than any religion, points to the UNITY OF THE WORLD...Perhaps, if we come to understand how modern physics, particularly quantum mechanics, can make us aware of the limits of human will, we will learn to GET ALONG WITH EACH OTHER...Even better, we may realize our cosmic heritage as part of the greater will.

　　– Dr. Fred Alan Wolfe, Taking the Quantum Leap

The full power of the Law of Attraction goes far beyond the acquisition of material things. This natural law has the potential to guide you to a truly successful, fulfilled life, one where you have IT All. BE clear on the life you want and the legacy you will leave behind. What is your intention? Ask for that! HAVE a high vibration and DO "in spirit" actions. These "in spirit" actions require the use of a finely tuned sixth and intuitive sense. It is a gift given to you and the time to use it is now. Practice the skills to master the Law of Attraction, taking yourself to ever higher levels of consciousness, beyond your desire for material abundance to experience true happiness through an abundant soul. You will become competent in attracting all you desire into your life — but there is so much more.

The discovery of quantum physics and its advancements over the past ten years is mind boggling. The "spooky" characteristics of the subatomic world seem to be present in the macro world. Science verifies the "Observer creating reality" applies not only to subatomic particles but to how you and I observe and create life around us. It also means "entanglement," a word quantum physicist Schroedinger coined to describe "the connection between vibrating entities," is as true at the macro or human level as it is at the subatomic level. It proves we are interconnected with all living things. It means the harm we are doing to the planet and to each other is experienced by and is killing all of us. The potentiality to use the science of quantum physics to create a new way of BEING, is moving at an exponential rate.

We are moving into a spiritual renaissance. There is evidence of a consciousness shift coming from far too many sources to ignore. Spirituality is about achieving a universal interconnectivity with our souls, discovering and fulfilling our life purpose. It is a process of evolution of consciousness destined to take us to a place of greater love, peace, and joy. You bring about that change in yourself by aspiring to live in love and abundance and, as you make the shift — the entire world changes — one enlightened soul at a time.

Awaken to the knowledge you create your world. We collectively create our external world through our intertwined thoughts and vibrations. If society holds a worldview of fear, scarcity, competition, and power, that is what manifests. The beautiful secret is we get to choose. Society can choose. The Law of Attraction teaches us how. If we choose personal thoughts of peace, joy, and abundance, we manifest that in our lives. If we choose a worldview of peace, joy, and abundance for all, collectively we can create that. We hold the key to unlock the potentiality of the Law of Attraction when we realize by connecting our thoughts and feelings with likeminded people, we ignite a powerful tsunami of change.

The time for that change is now.

With this awareness you are now part of a growing number of people who are inspired, enlightened, hopeful, and who have been jolted into action with startling, new, thought-provoking techniques and ideas to transform their reality. I encourage you to return to this material again and again. Each reading brings new insights. As you grow in awareness and begin to change, your eyes open to seeing new aspects in these thoughts. Our intention is a connection to the true source of success, fulfillment, and happiness. It is a journey to connect you to your soul or spirit — your soul abundant. Spirit journeys take time. Each milestone advances you to new levels of consciousness. The skills you pick up along the way enable you to master the natural Law of Attraction. Soon you become a Conscious Attractor.

What you are learning is leading edge. The timeframe you have to learn these skills is speeding up. Humanity needs enlightened people who are discovering their spiritual connection to each other and to nature. The Law of Attraction is one piece of knowledge to show you how to become "Soul Abundant." The time for change is NOW. Enlightened souls know they can create their reality and that reality can be a heaven on earth. What finer legacy than to be able to say you left, for your children and future generations, a more beautiful and loving place to live. We are the generation that created the greatest havoc on the planet. Yet more than any other generation in the history of civilization, we have what it takes, the intelligence, the technology, the know how, not only to clean up our mess but to transcend spiritually beyond our current narcissistic levels of consciousness and recreate a blissful garden to be shared by all.

Can we truly make such a huge change from where we are now to become a species capable of love and spirituality? Why not? If we can go from taking the first flight, to landing on the moon in just a few decades, anything is possible with our collective consciousness. Being more loving is the essence of learning to use the Law of Attraction. You begin by loving yourself. You begin by expressing gratitude and celebrating what is good in your life and realizing you are connected with every living thing on the planet. To attract goodness, you hold a high level of vibration or consciousness and project that vibration out into the world. Through entanglement, it mixes with like-energies and expands exponentially.

Create communities of likeminded people. Use your collective energy and thoughts to transform yourself, your community, and the world. Aspire to live in gratitude and abundance — then the entire world can change — one gratefully abundant soul at a time.

You will surely attract the things you currently define as essential for success — relationships, house, car, or finances — with the Soul Abundant method to the Law of Attraction. However, the true measure of success, the quest for higher consciousness is where you will find true happiness and fulfillment, and this quest never ends. Keep dreaming bigger dreams for yourself and for humanity and your soul will sing!

It is the dream in the process of unfolding that holds the vibrations to bring you success, fulfillment, and true happiness. This is the secret to success. You **IMAGINE YOUR SOUL ABUNDANT!**

Imagination is everything — it is the preview of life's coming attractions.
  – Albert Einstein

The time for success, fulfillment, and true happiness is right now. The time for spiritual awakening is right now. The time to evolve into our loving nature at One with All is right now. Who will participate in this consciousness movement?

If not you — who? Right now!

Five Insights
to the Law of Attraction

First Insight

We are interconnected energy with the power to create our world through our thoughts and feelings.

Second Insight

Live a life of non-duality seeking the best in, and for, yourself and all around you.

Third Insight

Seeking gratitude in all things opens the doors to higher consciousness and true life happiness.

Fourth Insight

The dream, in the process of unfolding, holds the vibration to create success, fulfillment, and true happiness. Always hold a dream.

Fifth Insight

When you "hear" or "feel" the little inner voice of your intuition, act in an "in spirit" way.

Appendix A
The Methods

Applied kinesiology

This technique is usually done with a partner, although there are some variations you can do alone. Doing it alone requires a level of expertise to ensure you are not influencing the result, so we recommend you begin to learn the technique using a partner.

When doing applied kinesiology with a partner, have one individual stand with an arm outstretched at shoulder level and exactly parallel to the floor. The tester faces the individual or can stand behind, placing a hand softly on one shoulder for balance and, with the opposite hand, use two fingers on the wrist of the subject's outstretched arm to apply pressure. When ready to conduct the test, the tester says, "Resist," and applies pressure to the arm. A strong arm indicates a "Yes" response; a weak arm indicates a "No" response. Only declarative statements with a "Yes" or "No" answer can be used for this testing.

It is not necessary for either of you to know the answer to what you are asking nor is it necessary to speak the words aloud. You can choose to just think the statement. This technique is connecting you intuitively with the universal knowledge of the energy field where all truth resides. You can seek any information you wish to know. The answers can only be a "Yes" or "No," and the request is made in the form of a declarative statement: "My name is Judy" not "Is my name Judy?"

Before you begin to use applied kinesiology to communicate with your inner voice or connect to universal energy, ensure you are well hydrated with good, clean water. It is also advisable to check if you and your partner are in alignment and if this is the right time for you to be doing energy work together. You ask, "I have permission to work with (name) as my universal compass."

Then proceed to apply pressure on the outstretched arm of your partner. If there is a weak response you may wish to do a thymus thump. (Refer to thymus section that follows.)

Then ask again. If there is still a weak response, this may not be a good candidate for you to work with right now. Stress, negative emotions, illness, or fatigue could all be factors. Change partners or test again on another day.

Begin to learn this technique by using some obviously healthful and non-healthful physical items. Test while having an individual hold an apple, you get a strong result. Test while holding a packet of sugar, especially an artificial sweetener, and you get a very weak test response.

Then test for a name. "My name is (your correct name)" and then "My name is (a false name)."

Testing for the positive or negative impact of physical items is the application of this technique developed by Dr. George Goodhart. Testing for intellectual truth such as your name or for emotional impact such as smiling or frowning at someone is typical of the research done by Dr. John Diamond. The person being tested is the one for whom we are seeking answers. They hold the physical item or make the statement, and someone else applies pressure to their outstretched arm.

Universal compass. In the technique to test concepts or ideas in the universal energy field, such as our intention statements, we use a slight variation on the technique. Someone else acts as your "compass" and their response provides your answers. Your partner provides their body for you to use to test the truth of your intention statements. Again, prior to starting, ask permission to conduct a test with this person and test for a positive response.

There is one caution with all testing. Anyone whose dominant vibration is negative, on the regressive, duality side of the Body Conscious guide with feelings of hopelessness, sadness, shame, guilt, grief, fear, doubt, or anger may be unable to get a valid test. The ideal is to remain as emotionally neutral as possible, not anticipating any particular result. Hold a thought of gratitude. Optimal results are obtained when working with people whose primarily vibration is on the progressive, non-duality side of the chart.

You can ask for insights or answers with this method and you can also validate the truth of your intention. As you developed your intention statement you clearly defined what you wanted. Then you started to shift from the left-brain thinking that may have dominated your writing of the list, to heart-centered or intuitive thinking, by reading your sentences for the feelings they triggered in your body. Any low feelings or low vibrational words were replaced. Next you visualized the words for the images they created.

Now, through applied kinesiology you can tap into your intuition to see if what you are asking is really in alignment with your Higher Self or inner self.

Assess the truth of your intention statement. Test each of your intention sentences. If you get a strong response, keep the wording as it is. If you get a spongy response, consider which words need to be changed.

I had a young man in one of my seminars who wanted to attract the ideal girlfriend. One of his statements was about her being slim. That statement was testing weak. By questioning him, we determined that the word slim could be intimidating if she was as thin as a model. So he changed the wording to "well-toned and athletic," and it tested strong. Another eleven-year-old girl wanted to be skinny. This word was testing weak for her. When she changed it to, "I am the perfect weight for my age and body," it tested strong and she was delighted.

At the end of the testing of your intention statements, you will test for "My list is complete." If it tests strong, you are finished. If it tests weak, you will test for "I need one more item" or "I need two more items," and so on. When you get a weak test go back to the previous number. For example, if one more item and two more items test strong, but three items tests weak, it means you need to add two more statements to your list to get the clarity you require.

The power of holding an intention

Another intriguing test is to demonstrate how powerful holding an intention can be. You can see through this simple test how you can deflect the impact of negative influences around you if you have a passionate intention.

Do the following test with a partner. Allow yourself to think very negative and hurtful thoughts about your partner. He or she will test weak. Now ask your partner to hold a very strong intention about something about which he or she is passionate. Again think the same negative and hurtful thoughts, but this time, the person will test strong!

When you conduct any applied kinesiology test, it is critical to complete the testing with the person in a strong state by testing with a positive thought or healthy object. Return to the person you have just conducted the above test with and hold loving thoughts. They will test strong.

Thymus thump

If you are getting an obviously incorrect reading, you can do one of two things. You can test the thymus gland or have the subject thump on their chest 10 to 12 times. This will "awaken" the gland and provide an accurate test.

If you decide to test for the strength of your thymus gland, place your fingertips on your skin at the point where the second rib connects with the breastbone which is the location of the thymus gland and where you will conduct the thymus thump. Use the standard applied kinesiology test.

Extend your arm parallel to the floor and have someone apply pressure. If you get a weak test, then proceed to do the thump on the chest 10 to 12 times. Test again. The test should be strong.

If the person being tested has a weak test for the thymus gland, it will affect all other testing, so use of the thymus thump is essential. Situations that can have a weakening effect are injury, stress, fatigue, or chronic degenerative illness. Low level vibrational emotions also weaken the thymus — emotions such as hate, envy, suspicion, and fear. Loving thoughts or emotions will strengthen the thymus. You can use loving thoughts, rather than the thymus thump, and you will get the same strong result.

Pendulum dowsing

Set up your pendulum by discovering the pendulum's neutral mode. To do this you sit comfortably, cross legged or with ankles crossed, and hold the pendulum in the center of your body between your knees and say, "Show me neutral position." Dangle the pendulum loosely between thumb, forefinger, and middle finger.

The pendulum may respond by being completely stationery or moving in a slight backward-and-forward movement. Then hold the pendulum over the right knee and say, "Show me 'Yes'." The pendulum, most often, will move in a clockwise direction. To find the "No" position, hold the pendulum over the left knee and say, "Show me 'No'." It should begin to move in a counter-clockwise direction. These are the most common responses. To test your responses, write "Yes" on a sheet of paper, hold the pendulum over the paper, speak the word YES, and record the movement of the pendulum. Repeat this for a "No" response. Finally, hold the pendulum between the legs again and say, "Show me 'Ask again'." Make a note of which response your pendulum wants to give you that is right for the pendulum, for you, and for your energy.

If your pendulum definitely shows something different than the most common clockwise for YES and counterclockwise for NO, let it do its own thing and accept these are the answers that are right for you and your pendulum, as long as they are being consistent.

Appendix B
Worksheet for
Intention Statement

INTENTION STATEMENT WORKSHEET

My intention to manifest _____

What I Don't Want | What I Do Want

Attracting Success

INTENTION STATEMENT

I am 100% committed to attracting all I need to BE, HAVE, DO to manifest

my intention for _____

Intention Sentences

Feel

Visualize

Applied Kinesiology

I am Grateful and ready to receive - right now!

Attracting Success

Bibliography

Arva, Virender Kumar. *The Book of the Vedas*. New York, NY: Barron's Educational Series, 2003.

Besant, Annie Wood. *Thought Power: Its Control and Culture*. New York, NY: Kessinger Publishing, 1996.

Brown, H. Jackson, Jr. *Live and Learn and Pass It On.*, Nashville, TN: Rutledge Hill Press, 1992.

Calleman, Carl Johan. *The Mayan Calendar and the Transformation of Consciousness*, Rocheser, VT: Bear & Company, 2004.

Chopra, Deepak. *Creating Affluence: The A-Z Steps to a Richer Life*. Novato, CA: New World Library, 1998.

Chopra, Deepak. "Why God Leaves Us Alone," *ODE Magazine*,Volume 5, Issue 1, Jan/Feb, 2007.

Diamond, John. *Your Body Doesn't Lie*. New York, NY: Warner Books, 1979.

Dyer, Wayne. *Inspiration: Your Ultimate Calling*. Carlsbad, CA: Hay House, 2006.

Dyer, Wayne. *Ten Secrets for Success and Inner Peace*. Carlsbad, CA: Hay House, 2001.

Dyer, Wayne. *The Power of Intention: Learning to Co-create Your World Your Way*. Carlsbad, CA: Hay House, 2004.

Eason, Cassandra. *The Art of the Pendulum*. York Beach, ME: Red Wheel/Weiser, 2005.

Edwards, Tony. "Dowsing: Is It a Field Effect?" in *Living the Field: A Master Class for Living in the New Age*. London, UK: Satellite House (lesson five, pages 2–4).

Edwards, Tony. "The Ancient Art of the Pendulum" in *Living the Field: A Master Class for Living in the New Age*. London, UK: Satellite House (lesson 5, pages 2–6).

Edwards, Tony. "The Fine Art of Meditation" in *Living the Field: A Master Class for Living in the New Age*. London, UK: Satellite House (lesson seven, pages 2–4).

Eker, Harv T. *Speedwealth: How to Make a Million In Your Own Business in Three Years Or Less*. Canada: Peak Potentials Publishing, 1996.

Gladwell, Malcolm. *Blink: The Power of Thinking Without Thinking*. New York, NY: Little, Brown and Company, 2005.

Grabhorn, Lynn. *Excuse Me Your Life is Waiting*. Charlottesville, VA: Hampton Roads Publishing, 2000.

Gregory, Eva. *The Feel Good Guide to Prosperity*. San Franscisco, CA: Leading Edge Publishers, 2004.

Gyatso, Geshe Kelsang. *The New Meditation Handbook*. Glen Spey, NY: Tharpa Publications, 2001.

Hawkins, David R. *The Eye of the I: From Which Nothing Is Hidden*. W. Sedona, AZ: Veritas Publishing, 2001.

Hawkins, David R. *I: Reality and Subjectivity*. W. Sedona, AZ: Veritas Publishing, 2003.

Hawkins, David R. *Power vs Force: The Hidden Determinants of Human Behavior.*, Carlsbad, CA: Hay House, 2002.

Hawkins, David R. *Transcending the Levels of Consciousness: The Stairway to Enlightenment*. W. Sedona, AZ: Veritas Publishing, 2006.

Hawkins, David R. *Truth vs Falsehood: How To Tell The Difference*. Toronto, Canada: Axial Publishing Company, 2005.

Helmstetter, Shad. *What To Say When You Talk To Yourself: Powerful New Techniques to Program Your Potential for Success*. Scottsdale, AZ: Grindle Press, 1982.

Hicks, Esther and Hicks, Jerry. *The Amazing Power of Deliberate Intent*. Carlsbad, CA: Hay House, 2006.

Hicks, Esther and Hicks, Jerry. *Ask and It Is Given*. Carlsbad, CA: Hay House, 2004.

Hill, Napoleon. *Grow Rich!: With Peace of Mind*. Los Angeles, CA: Highroads Media, 1996.

Hill, Napoleon. *Think and Grow Rich*. Los Angeles, CA: Highroads Media, 2004.

Hunt, Valerie V. *Infinite Mind: Science of the Human Vibrations of Consciousness*. Malibu, CA: Malibu Publishing, 1996.

Kurzweil, Ray. *The Age of Spiritual Machines: When Computers Exceed Human Intelligence*. New York, NY: Penguin, 1999.

Kurzweil, Ray and Grossman, Terry. *Fantastic Voyage: Live Long Enough To Live Forever*. USA: Rodale, 2004.

Langemeier, Loral. *The Millionaire Maker*. New York, NY: McGraw-Hill, 2006.

Leadbeater, C.W. *Some Glimpses of Occultism*. New York, NY: Kessinger Publishing, 2003.

Lipton, Bruce. *The Biology of Belief*. Santa Rosa, CA: Mountain of Love/Elite Books, 2005.

Losier, Michael. *Law of Attraction: The Science of Attracting More of What You Want and Less of What You Don't*. Author, 2004.

Mails, Thomas E. *The Hopi Survival Kit*. New York, NY: Penguin, 1997.

Mandino, Og. *The Greatest Mystery in the World*. New York, NY: Ballantine Books, 1997.

Mandino, Og. *Og Mandino's University of Success*. New York, NY: Bantam Books, 1982.

McTaggart, Lynne. "The Electric Power of our Intention" in *Living the Field: A Master Class for Living in the New Age*. London, UK: Satellite House (lesson eight, page 5).

McTaggart, Lynne. *The Field: The Quest for the Secret Force f the Universe*. New York, NY: HarperCollins, 2002.

McTaggart, Lynne. "How Strong is Our Intention?" in *Living the Field: A Master Class for Living in the New Age*. London, UK: Satellite House (lesson two, pages 12–13).

McTaggart, Lynne. *The Intention Experiment: Use Your Thoughts to Change the World*. Hammersmith, UK: HarperElement, 2007.

McTaggart, Lynne. "The Power of Intention," *ODE Magazine*, Volume 5, Issue 1 Jan/Feb, 2007.

Myss, Caroline. *Anatomy of the Spirit: The Seven Stages of Power and Healing*. New York, NY: Three Rivers Press, 1997.

Myss, Caroline. *Sacred Contracts: Awakening Your Divine Potential*. New York, NY: Three Rivers Press, 2003.

Nightengale, Earl. *Lead the Field*. Niles, IL: Nightingale-Conant, n.d.

Pert, Candace B. *Molecules of Emotion: The Science behind Mind-Body Medicine*. New York, NY: Scribner, 1997.

Proctor, Bob. *You Were Born Rich*. Scottsdale, AZ: LifeSuccess Productions, 1997.

Radin, Dean. *Entangled Minds: Extrasensory Experiences in a Quantum Reality*. New York, NY: Pocket Books, 2006.

Rann Michale C. and Rann Arrott, Elizabeth. *Shortcut to a Miracle: How to Change Your Consciousness and Transform Your Life*. Santa Monica, CA: Jeffers Press, 2005.

Secretan, Lance. *Inspire: What Great Leaders Do!* Hoboken, NJ: John Wiley & Sons, 2004.

Simic, Vesela. "The Challenge of Forgiveness," *SHIFT Magazine*, Number 13, Dec 2006/Feb 2007.

Talbot, Michael. *The Holographic Universe.* New York, NY: HarperPerennial, 1992.

Tarnas, Richard. *Cosmos and Psyche.* New York, NY: Penguin, 2006.

Tolle, Eckart. *A New Earth.* New York, NY: Penguin, 2005.

Vitale, Joe. *The Attractor Factor: Five Easy Steps For Creating Wealth (Or Anything Else) From The Inside Out.* Hoboken, NJ: Wiley, 2005.

Vitale, Joe. *Spiritual Marketing.* Author, 2001.

Walsh, Neale Donald. *The New Revelations: A Conversation with God.* New York, NY: Atria Books, 2002.

Walsh, Neale Donald. "God is Dead! Long live God!" *ODE Magazine,* Volume 5, Issue 2, March, 2007.

Wattles, Wallace. *The Science of Getting Rich.* Largo, FL: Top of the Mountain Publishing, 2002.

Wolf, Fred Alan. *Taking the Quantum Leap: The New Physics for Non-Scientists.* New York, NY: Harper & Row Publishers, 1989.

Wheatley, Margaret J. *Leadership and the New Science.* San Francisco, CA: Berrett-Koehler Publishers, 1999.

Wilkinson, Bruce. *The Dream Giver.* Sisters, OR: Multnomah Publishers, 2003.

Zohar, Danah and Marshall, Ian. *Spiritual Capital: Wealth We Can Live By.* San Francisco, CA: Berrett-Koehler Publishers, 2004.

Zukav, Gary. *Dancing Wu Li Master: An Overview of the New Physics*. New York, NY: Bantam, 1984.

Zukav, Gary and Francis, Linda. *The Heart of the Soul: Emotional Awareness*. New York, NY: Simon & Schuster, 2001.

ABOUT THE AUTHOR

What are the essential ingredients for success? In 2000, Judy Berg came to a point in her marketing career that left her full of doubt. She had enjoyed rapid advancement in her careers in executive management, communications, and leadership training, but now was left questioning why success worked easily for some and yet eluded others who worked so diligently.

Judy stepped into senior management in her first job in a children's hospital after graduating from the University of Alberta. That level of corporate leadership became the norm for her later appointments throughout her fifteen year career in the Canadian federal government. When she left government to test her skills in entrepreneurship, she again quickly attained a leadership position in her network marketing company. It was here she began to observe success was more dependent upon attitudes, thoughts, and feelings than upon skills and actions. Success was about consciousness, awareness, and intention.

Now she realized her consciousness, in the form of an unwavering positive belief, more than her skills, had been the key to her success. She immersed herself in a study of quantum physics, consciousness, intention, and the Law of Attraction. Using her well-honed training skills, and with the encouragement of her colleagues, she developed the Attracting Success seminars and then founded Soul Abundant.com, a company dedicated to promoting a consciousness-driven life. The Soul Abundant seminars are highly rated by participants in Canada and the US. Intention and intuition are guiding principles in her life.

She and her husband, Jim, spend their time in Canada and Australia, fulfilling their intention to travel and share in the lives of their son, Regan, a resident surgeon in Canada, and daughter, Markail, her husband, Stuart, and their infant son in Australia. Judy is available for speaking engagements and seminars and can be reached through her website at www.soulabundant.com.